PROJECT TITLE: DESIGN AND IMPLEMENTATION OF THE REMOTE CONTROL SYSTEM USING SMS VIA GSM FOR HOME ELECTRICAL SYSTEM (REMC-HOUSE)

By Mr.Kadeghe Fue and Dr. Charles Tarimo

STATEMENT OF AUTHORSHIP AND ORIGINALITY

I declare that this report and the work described in it are my own work, with any Contributions from others expressly acknowledged and/or cited.

I declare that the work in this report was carried out in accordance with the Regulations of the University of Dar es Salaam and has not been presented to any other University for Examination either in Tanzania or overseas. Any views expressed in the report are those of the author and in no way represent those of the University of Dar es Salaam.

ABSTRACT

In this project, an attempt is made to extend the flexibility provided by mobile phones in interpersonal communication to be applicable in electrical/electronic systems control. As two people in two different geographical locations can communicate using mobile phone, it would be of interest if this same communication system can be used by one to control the operation of electrical/electronic appliances remotely.

To utilize the aforementioned opportunity, the Remote control system using SMS via GSM network for home electrical system (REMC-HOUSE) has been proposed. With the implementation of the REMC-HOUSE, user could easily control the electrical devices remotely. The REMC-HOUSE consists of phone, modem and computer. The three have been integrated such that they can be used to control electrical/electronic appliances in a home/house remotely.

The circuit has a microcontroller that controls the devices like fans and lights. Also the PC is employed to translate the SMS that are received from the GSM modem. The GSM modem is used to send and receive SMS. The intended user should have the handset that can send and receive SMS.

The System software could save the messages sent to it for a particular time before the user restarts the system. These sessions that are saved are essential for further analysis of the system users' behavior. The system detects anonymous SMS while saving it in logs and sends back a warning to the authorized and unauthorized user.

The system software provides the capability to record all the activities done by a super user (here referred as administrator). These reports can be generated as grid view or in Excel spreadsheet for further analysis of the user behaviors to the system.

The system software provides a relevant sms reports to the administrator about users who violates the system's services. Also, the software is capable of sensing lack of electricity hence giving out the reports. Also its gives a user to remotely shut down the system to prevent it from fatal shut down.

Generally, circuit part properties comprise only 25% of the REMC Technology. 75% is covered by an advanced software properties as described above.

ACKNOWLEDGEMENT

First of all, On behalf of the University of Dar es Salaam, College of Information and Communication Technologies (CoICT), Department of Computer Science and Engineering, I wish to extend my heartfelt gratitude to Sokoine University of Agriculture for giving the opportunity to me to conduct my research in electrical systems and microcontrollers.

I am extending my heartfelt gratitude to Professor Siza Tumbo for hosting me in his Laboratory (Instrumentation, control and Micro-computer Lab) at SUA for more than 4 weeks. At those Labs I was able to test and experiment control, electrical systems and microcontrollers. In addition, I was able to develop my project entitled Electrical Power control system using SMS that covers concepts for REMC-HOUSE system.

I am extending my heartfelt gratitude to Dr. C. Tarimo for being my supervisor in this final year project especially for guiding me on progressive work and report writing.

Furthermore, I also extend my sincere thanks to Mrs. C. Kilasara for providing valuable information to me on using the devices in the laboratory. I would like to express my thanks to all the people at SUA Engineering department who made my stay very pleasant and comfortable and for all the hospitality extended to me.

Finally, an honorable mention goes to my family and friends for their understandings and supports on me in completing my final year Project work especially financially and psychologically. Without their helps, I would have faced many difficulties while doing this training.

TABLE OF CONTENTS

STATEMENT OF AUTHORSHIP AND ORIGINALITY i
ABSTRACT ii
ACKNOWLEDGEMENT iii
LIST OF FIGURES v
LIST OF ABBREVIATION vi
CHAPTER 1 1
1. INTRODUCTION 1
   1.1. BACKGROUND AND GENERAL OVERVIEW 1
   1.2. PROBLEM STATEMENT 2
   1.3. OBJECTIVES 2
      1.3.1. Main Objective 2
      1.3.2. Specific Objectives: 2
   1.4. PROJECT SCOPE 3
CHAPTER 2 4
2. LITERATURE REVIEW 4
CHAPTER 3 9
3. METHODOLOGY 9
CHAPTER 4 11
   4.1. GENERAL SYSTEM DESCRIPTIONS 11
      4.1.1. Product perspective 11
      4.1.4. Operating Environment 12
      4.1.5. Assumption and dependencies 12
   4.2. REQUIREMENTS ELICITATION 12
      4.2.1. Functional Requirements 12
      4.2.2. Non-Functional Requirements 13
   4.3. SYSTEM ANALYSIS 17
   4.4. SYSTEM FEATURES AND DESIGN 18
      4.4.1. Modem Features 18
      4.4.2. Electronic Circuit Features 18

- 4.4.3. REMC-HOUSE SOFTWARE FEATURES 21
  - 4.4.3.1. Connect to the modem and Microcontroller::SF01 21
  - 4.4.3.2. System Feature Show REMC "About" information::SF02 22
  - 4.4.3.3. System Feature current session information::SF03 22
  - 4.4.3.4. System Feature Message sent to Microcontroller::SF04 22
  - 4.4.3.5. System Feature Notified unauthorized user::SF05 22
  - 4.4.3.6. System Feature set a authorized numbers::SF07 23
  - 4.4.3.7. System Feature saves users numbers::SF08 23
  - 4.4.3.8. System Feature Request for last message status::SF09 23
- 4.5. IMPLEMENTATION 30
- 4.6. SYSTEM TESTING 41

CHAPTER 5 43

5. CONCLUSIONS 43
   - 5.1. USER REQUIREMENTS 43
   - 5.2. EFFECTIVENESS 43
   - 5.3. LEARNABILITY 43
   - 5.4. RECOMMENDATIONS 43
   - 5.5. CONCLUSION EVALUATION 43
6. REFERENCE 44
7. APPENDIX 45
   - A. FORM: QUESTIONNAIRE FOR REMC HOUSE SYSTEM 45
   - B. TIME SCHEDULE OF Phase II 46
   - C. TIME SCHEDULE OF Phase I 47

LIST OF FIGURES

Figure 1 : graph that shows PWM signal 7
Figure 2 : show the context diagram for the REMC-HOUSE 11
Figure 3: use case diagram 14
Figure 4: uml class diagram for remc 17
Figure 5 : ZX-328n Circuit configuration 19
Figure 6: Serial comm. interface for ZX-328n Microcontroller 20
Figure 7 : PWM Solenoid/Valve driver configuration circuit 21
Figure 8 : common database architecture 24
Figure 9 : sequence diagram for administrator login 25
Figure 10 : receiving and sending SMS 26
Figure 11: sequence diagram for starting the system 26
Figure 12 : Design class diagram for starting the system 27
Figure 13 : design class diagram for administrative updates 28
Figure 14 : system's ERD 29
Figure 15: System's XML Template ERD 29
Figure 16 : REMC House electronic circuit 30
Figure 17: login form for starting the system 32
Figure 18 : invalid login warning 32
Figure 19 : start system module that connects the modem and the circuit 33
Figure 20 : the admin form displaying the admin number settings 34
Figure 21 : login form for administrator 34
Figure 22 : administrative form for system service options 35
Figure 23 : user interruption table or sessions 35
Figure 24 : command table and updates form 36
Figure 25 : invalid change when performed 36
Figure 26: Attempt to add new administrators 37
Figure 27: accessing the master login functionality of the system 38
Figure 28: Exporting admin sessions to excel file 39
Figure 29: Excel 2007 sheet for admin sessions 40
Figure 30 : remc database in phpmyadmin 41

LIST OF ABBREVIATION

BTS: Base Telecommunication station..4

GSM: Global service for mobile communication..1

JAD: Joint Application Development...12

REMC -HOUSE: Remote control system using SMS via GSM for home electrical system.........................1

SMS: Short Message Service...1

SP: Service Pack..9

TANESCO: Tanzania Electrical Supply Company..1

USB: Universal Serial Port...9

CHAPTER 1

1. INTRODUCTION

1.1. BACKGROUND AND GENERAL OVERVIEW

The term **GSM** explain the communication in general, it stand for Global System for Mobile communication. The mobile communication it refers to the playing field of communication that gives communication in motion.

The term (**SMS**) Short Message Service is the text communication service component of phone, web or mobile communication systems, using standardized communications protocols that allow the exchange of short text messages between fixed line or mobile phone devices. SMS text messaging is the most widely used data application in the world, with 2.4 billion active users, or 74% of all mobile phone subscribers. The SMS will be sent from the modem using the AT commands. Common AT commands include AT+CMGS (send message), AT+CMSS (send message from storage), AT+CMGL (list messages) and AT+CMGR (read message).

A remote control is an electronic device that is used to control other devices distantly. Most commonly known remote control is like that of the television that needs a line of sight to control TV. REMC needs only SMS to control the electrical devices from distant.

In homes, Electricity is used to power furnaces, light fixtures, appliances and many other electrical devices. Electricity is sent to a house from the utility company (TANESCO) through overhead power lines and/or underground conduits sometimes. This power is delivered most commonly through three main lines, called three-wire service. This is the type of energy delivery system that most households have. There are two "hot" wires, which each deliver 220-240 volts of electricity, and one neutral wire. Most household lights and appliances use 20-100 watts, only requiring the use of one hot wire. However, larger appliances and electrical devices, such as air conditioners, electric ovens and furnaces may require relative high electricity. All electrical circuits require the presence of the neutral line. So the device needs a valve or solenoid that will be used to control these high volts of the appliances and that the signal sent from the microcontroller.

1.2. PROBLEM STATEMENT

Situations that call for a capability to be controlled remotely are many and varied. For example, a home owner might need to switch ON/OFF some of the electrical appliance at home when he/she is away. Although, already there are many types of remote controls being used to control various electronic devices/appliances in home, most of these remote control are limited by range and/or the requirement of line of sight. Nevertheless, the existing remote controls give us flexibility and comfort in controlling the appliances from a distance.

Given the shortfall of the existing home appliance remote controls, then this project sets out to address this shortfall by proposing a remote control based on the GSM technology. With the availability of the GSM networks new types of remote controls can be devised that make use of the GSM to improve the range (distance) and flexibility of controlling appliances. Since, GSM is not affected by the line of sight so long as there is network coverage. And then, we hope the system would extend the range and flexibility of controlling certain home electric/electronic appliances.

1.3. OBJECTIVES

1.3.1. Main Objective
The project is to equip a home owner with flexibility of controlling some of his/her electrical/electronic appliances at home remotely i.e. when he/she is away from home.

1.3.2. Specific Objectives:
To link GSM network with home electrical/electronic system by developing;

i. The software that utilizes the SMS and software interfaces both electronic circuit and modem.

ii. An electronic circuit and its interfaces with computer(serial communication) and its connections with the electrical devices

iii. System has to generate reports and spreadsheets for all the events and sessions that occurring in the system. Such events like sms sent/received, administrator updates to the system and more. This allows system to be easily audited.

iv. A flexible system that gives report to the administrator for abnormalities. Also, the system that senses absence of electricity so as to be shut down remotely.

1.4. PROJECT SCOPE

The project focuses only on the few electrical appliances. The lights represent all devices that need a constant voltage supplier while the fans represent the devices that need pulses and varying voltages. Hence the project output only allows lighting and switching the fans.

CHAPTER 2

2. LITERATURE REVIEW

In achieving the above objectives, I had to review all the matter related to system while concurrently hypothesizing the project.

i. Reviewing the background of the problem and its' the current status in our country. The current existing systems that are mostly deployed in BTS. **Base transceiver station (BTS)** or **cell site** is a piece of equipment that facilitates wireless communication between user equipment (UE) and a network. For Airtel Company, they are produced by INALA from South Africa. They are well known as Asset management systems.

ii. Studying new tools like ZBASIC language, VB.NET 2008 language and AT commands.

- **Visual Basic (VB)** is the third-generation event-driven programming language and integrated development environment (IDE) from Microsoft for its COM programming model. Visual Basic is relatively easy to learn and use. Visual Basic was derived from BASIC and enables the rapid application development (RAD) of graphical user interface (GUI) applications, access to databases using Data Access Objects, Remote Data Objects, or ActiveX Data Objects, and creation of ActiveX controls and objects. Scripting languages such as VBA and VBScript are syntactically similar to Visual Basic, but perform differently. A programmer can put together an application using the components provided with Visual Basic itself. Programs written in Visual Basic can also use the Windows API, but doing so requires external function declarations. I am using the VB.NET 2008.

    Visual Basic .NET (VB.NET) is an object-oriented computer programming language that can be viewed as an evolution of the classic Visual Basic (VB) which is implemented on the .NET Framework. Microsoft currently supplies two major implementations of Visual Basic: Microsoft Visual Studio, which is commercial software and Microsoft Visual Studio Express, which is free of charge.

- The ZBasic language was designed to be highly compatible with Microsoft's Visual Basic (VB6) and with Net Media's BasicX; it is a subset of the former and a superset of the latter. The fundamental capabilities of these languages are augmented with carefully chosen extensions. The result is a powerful and easy-to-use language for microcontroller programming. If you're an experienced programmer, you'll find ZBasic a snap to pick up. And, if you've never written a computer program before you'll likely be pleased with how quick and easy it is to learn.
- AT commands are instructions used to control a modem. AT is the abbreviation of ATtention. Every command line starts with "AT" or "at". That's why modem commands are called AT commands. Many of the commands that are used to control wired dial-up modems, such as ATD (Dial), ATA (Answer), ATH (Hook control) and ATO (Return to online data state), are also supported by GSM/GPRS modems and mobile phones. Besides this common AT command set, GSM/GPRS modems and mobile phones support an AT command set that is specific to the GSM technology, which includes SMS-related commands like AT+CMGS (Send SMS message), AT+CMSS (Send SMS message from storage), AT+CMGL (List SMS messages) and AT+CMGR (Read SMS messages).

iii. Studying circuitry of ATMEL microcontrollers like ATMEGA ZX328-n. These are the high-performance; low-power Atmel 8-bit AVR RISC-based microcontroller combines 128KB of programmable flash memory, 4KB SRAM, a 4KB EEPROM, an 8-channel 10-bit A/D converter, and a JTAG interface for on-chip debugging. The device supports throughput of 16 MIPS at 16 MHz and operates between 4.5-5.5 volts.

iv. Reviewing on how to interface electronics circuit using the serial communication through internet and some relevant books written on serial communications.

v. Pulse Width modulation, abbreviated as PWM, is a method of transmitting information on a series of pulses. The data that is being transmitted is encoded on the width of these pulses to control the amount of power being sent to a load. In other words, pulse width modulation is a modulation technique for generating variable width pulses to represent the amplitude of an input analog signal or wave. The popular applications of pulse width modulation are in power delivery, voltage regulation and amplification and audio effects.

Pulse width modulation is used to reduce the total power delivered to a load without resulting in loss, which normally occurs when a power source is limited by a resistive element. The underlying principle in the whole process is that the average power delivered is directly proportional to the modulation duty cycle. If the modulation rate is high, it is possible to smooth out the pulse train using passive electronic filters and recover an average analog wave form.

High frequency pulse width modulation power control systems can be realized using semiconductor switches. Here, the discrete ON or OFF state of the modulation itself can be used to control the switches, thereby controlling the voltage or current across the load. The major advantage with these types of switches is that the voltage drop across it during conducting and non-conducting states is ideally zero. PWM's field of application includes Class D audio amplifiers, DC motor speed control, and light dimmers common in homes. Pulse width modulation is widely used in voltage regulators. It works by switching the voltage to the load with the appropriate duty cycle; the output will maintain a voltage at the desired level.

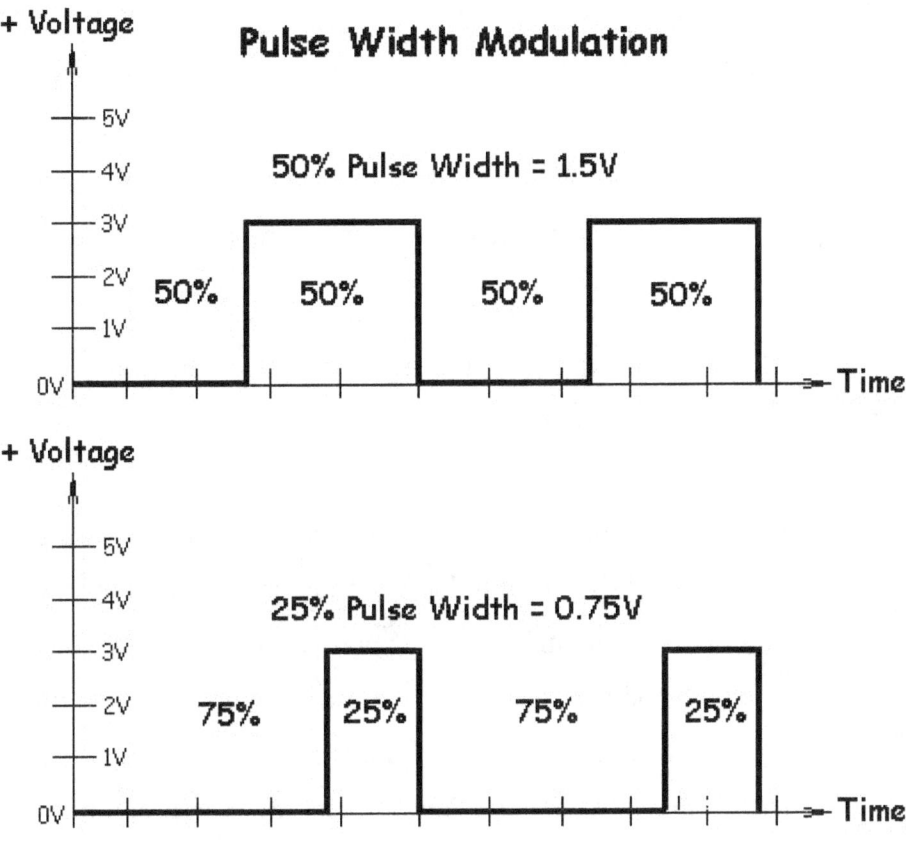

Figure 1 : graph that shows PWM signal

It's possible to achieve PWM signal using the microcontroller and run the fan.

vi. Object-orientation provides concepts, notations and methods for producing a model of a system. The use object-orientated principles and notations in any of the models may simplify the software development as object oriented notations are fairly expressive and therefore can express models that are closer to what has to be modeled from the real world therefore notations and methods are the core of all software engineering practice in real life. The expressiveness of object-orientation also facilitates a dense notation of models, which again makes it easier for consumers of models to understand and digest them. The most important feature of object-oriented is that it supports the important principle of information hiding such that design decisions that are local to a certain part of the model can be kept local and be hidden from the outside and can be changed without interfering with other parts of the model. Advantages of Object Oriented Modeling technique are:

- Object-oriented system supports re-use of objects, hence Implementation is simplified

- Phase Object-Oriented Methodology makes the system more flexible; since it collects separate modules then system maintenance is easy

Unified Modeling language (UML) is a standard language for specifying, analyzing, designing and documenting artifacts of an object-oriented software-intensive system under development. It is a language that has its roots in object-oriented modeling. UML uses diagrams in documenting systems.
I have chosen UML because I am too familiar with it. Also, since REMC is implemented in vb.net which is object oriented programming language.

CHAPTER 3

3. METHODOLOGY

i. An intensive reading through different literature and internet was done in order to achieve the objective set. The following has been done;
- Reading books and documents about GSM networks
- How to interface the GSM network to computer and send SMS through computer
- How to interface microcontrollers to computer specifically using the serial communication

ii. There are present related works that need to be revised. Such systems like the remote controllers based on radio frequencies.

iii. Collection of relevant data for the intended system e.g. Questionnaires and interviews.

iv. Analysis of the collected data and prioritizing the needs for the system

v. System design involves
- Object oriented programming which the program flow is determined by objects and classes.
- Designing the circuit for integration with the home electrical systems.
- Interfacing all the modules modem, computer, and circuit and home electrical devices.

vi. The system testing involves all the modules connected and the user sends a message and sees how the system responds to the interrupt. The system is able to respond after being asked to deliver something like switching on or off or sending back an SMS to the user.

vii. The system user manual preparation involves preparing a document that explains about system functionalities. This document is somehow equivalent to the help section of the software. There are two approaches of user guide. There is one that is found from online help of the REMC and another one located locally.

viii. Preparation of the system maintenance document and measurement of its usability, portability and durability. Since the system is had a shallow system testing then these parameters where not met as intended. Further analysis of the parameters is quite needed.

ix. Preparation of the electrical safety document. This REMC system has a circuit that needs a constant and reliable power adapter. Also in case it happens short-circuit then its reparability procedures. The REMC House is created as the model so partial electrical safety rules were observed during its design. This doesn't mean that it's prone to electricity short circuits abnormalities since REMC Circuit body is connected to a well tested power adapter that is capable of preventing power surges and other abnormalities.

CHAPTER 4

4.1. GENERAL SYSTEM DESCRIPTIONS

4.1.1. Product perspective

The REMC-House system does not work independently. It works together with the home computer, the software run in them and GSM network used by a modem.

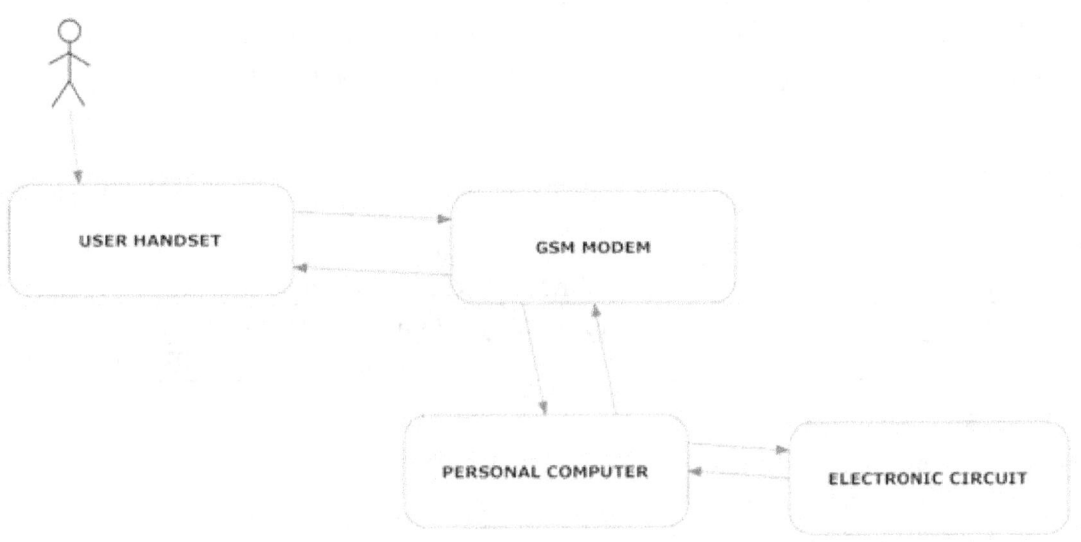

Figure 2 : show the context diagram for the REMC-HOUSE

4.1.2. Interfaces on the REMC-HOUSE network system

Communication interface

The REMC-HOUSE communicates with the user via a communication network (GSM). The messages sent via the communication network are specific to target remc-house or user handset.

Software interface

The software runs on a computer that connects between modem and electronic circuit.

Hardware interface

The hardware is connected using the serial communication techniques

User interfaces

User: User interface is user-friend such that a client could interrupt with the system without any assistance.

User Connect: interface that allows the user to add or change phone number. And connect the whole system using the port number attached to the computer.

User Sessions: This allows user to see the current sessions taken by a machine.

4.1.3. User characteristics

There are several registered users that interrupt with system:
- Users are simply legitimate members of the house.
- User doesn't have any need to have special education or experience.
- Maintainers must be experienced REMC-house computer engineer or expert.

4.1.4. Operating Environment

Particulars	System features
Operating System	Windows XP, VISTA and 7
Processor	Preferably 1.6Ghz but not necessary
Machine Serial Port	1 DB9 Comm. port and USB port

4.1.5. Assumption and dependencies

Assumptions about input, and/or environmental behavior
- hardware never fails as it operates constantly
- limited number of requests of users per day
- limited replies of users per day
- REMC-HOUSE computer and modem are online all the time.

4.2. REQUIREMENTS ELICITATION

4.2.1. Functional Requirements
- Lighting ON/OFF the LEDs using the electronic circuit
- Switch ON(1,2,3) and OFF(0) the fans using the electronic circuit
- Receiving request SMS from user and processing it
- Sending SMS reply to the user and reporting any misuse
- Interface between modem and PC that is so smooth
- Validation of
  - Legitimate user
  - Reporting and saving session interrupts
- Sending Error messages to the legitimate messages

4.2.2. Non-Functional Requirements
- Performance: The system is performing well when run in XP.
- Reliability/Availability: The system is readily reliable and well working if constant electricity is available
- Policy: The system abides with the government law and safety precautions in handling electrical devices.
- Security: The system use unique numbers and codes to secure the system from unauthorized users.
- Maintainability: The system has documentation for manual and maintenance procedures and techniques.

Elicitation techniques used

4.2.2.1. Use Cases
Use case describes interaction between the User, user device (User handset) and the electronic circuit. REMC House has typical relationships between its actors and use cases.

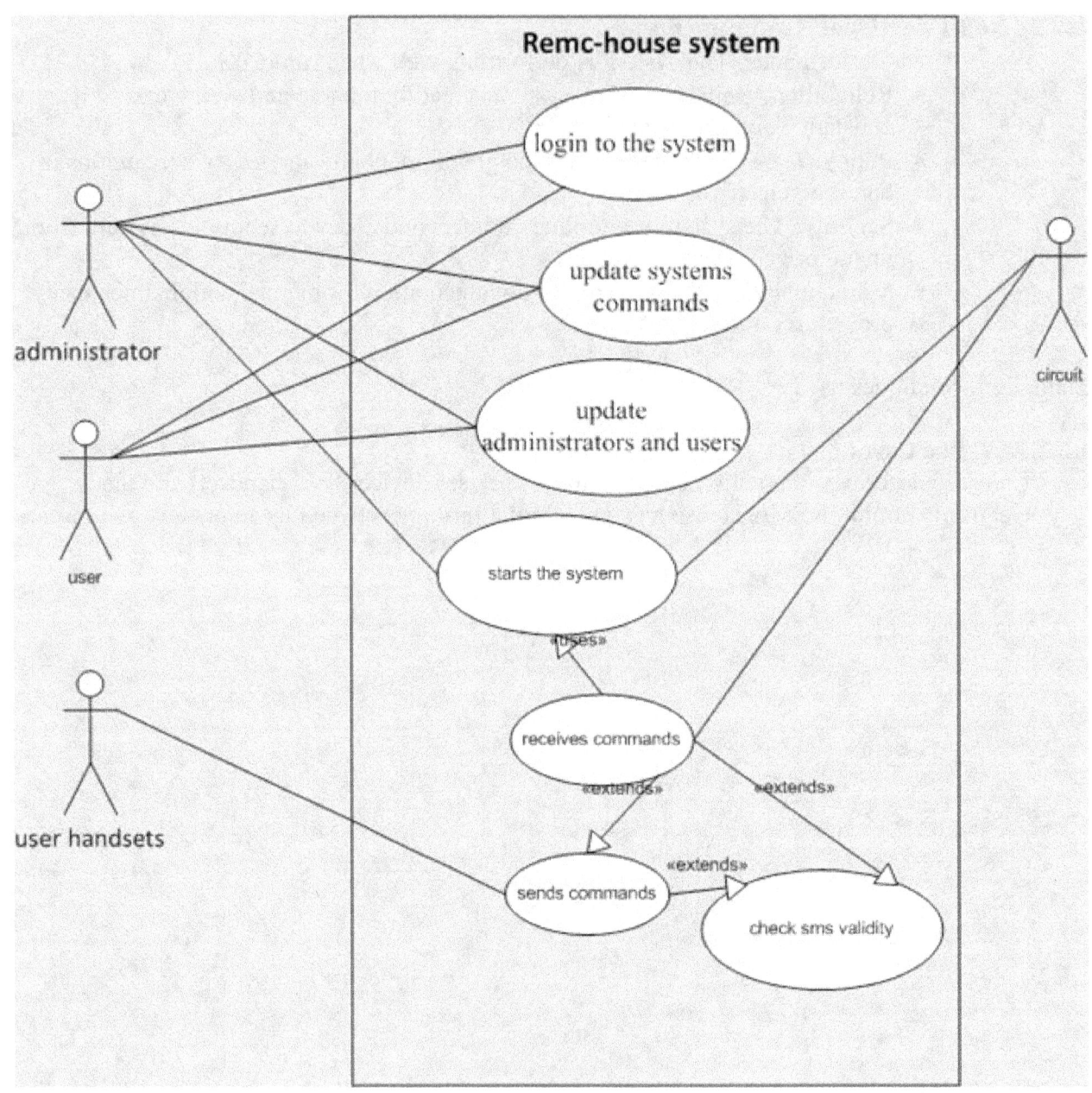

Figure 3: use case diagram

System actors

Actor	Description
Administrator	This is the most privileged user who can login into server of the database Roles; 1. Login into server 2. Starts the system 3. Stops the system. 4. Generally executes all the roles of the user 1. Can add new administrators and users

	2. Can login remotely 3. Can change the commands to the circuit 4. Can view all reports in sessions and events 5. Add new user handset
user	This is the registered user to use the system using the handset
User hand-set	This actor can only send and receive SMS 1. Can send SMS 2. Can receive SMS from the system
Circuit	This actor can only receive SMS message and send back its current status

Usecase

Usecase: Login

Description	The system should be able to control different access levels by capturing username and password of the user and comparing with that stored in the system's database in order to allow user perform legal access in the system.
Actors	Administrator
assumption	They have username and password set to the system.
scenario	1. System displays login page 2. User enter username and password then clicks login button 3. The system verifies the username and password entered.

Usecase: Update system commands

description	Allows the administrator or user to change the commands
Actors	Administrator, users
assumption	Login was successfully
Scenario	1. System displays the available commands 2. The system allows the commands to be changed, deleted or added new ones

Usecase: Update administrator and users

description	Allows the administrator or user to change the administrator and users
actors	Administrator

assumption	Login was successfully
scenario	1. System displays the available administrators and users 2. The system allows the admin and user to be changed, deleted or added new ones

Usecase: Starts the system

description	Allows the administrator to start the system
actors	Administrator
assumption	Login was successfully
scenario	1. System displays the start form 2. The system allows the admin to start the system 3. Checks if the admin has already started the system or it starts automatically under acceptance of the administrator

Usecase: Sms validity

description	System checks the validity of the SMS
actors	User handset
assumption	1. Login was successfully 2. The message is received
scenario	1. System checks if the sender number is available in the system 2. Checks also the commands if available in the system

4.2.2.2. Questionnaire Method

I fetched the information by using both open-ended and close-ended Questionnaires. This is the sample of my close-ended and open-ended questionnaire I used. I gathered this information from my fellow students and to some house owners in Dar es Salaam and Morogoro. *Refer to appendix.*

4.2.2.3. Requirements gathering sessions(JAD)

I gathered information about security by talking and asking expected users and my fellow students for REMC-House. How the PIN and other security should be implemented. They suggested using integer number instead of using a word to send request machine. This prevents a lost handset to be used by a thief to instruct/command the system.
Also, I was able to gather information of the interface like colors, forms of the REMC-House software. The users needed to see that it's a flexible program that could run in a low cost

computer that they needed to use. Also, they suggested to use a windows OS instead of UNIX system as many didn't know them.

I discussed with them the way to display several messages on the REMC-HOUSE systems. Examples of these messages include message when the system is out of service, network is down, request received, system has failed, legitimacy of the SMS, the saving of the sessions, System replies SMS etc.

4.3. SYSTEM ANALYSIS
4.3.1. The UML Class Diagram

Class diagram shows a set of classes, interfaces and collaborations and their relationships; a class diagram addresses the static design view of a system, it is a diagram that shows a collection of static elements. A class is a description of the set of objects that share the same attributes operations, relationships, and semantics.

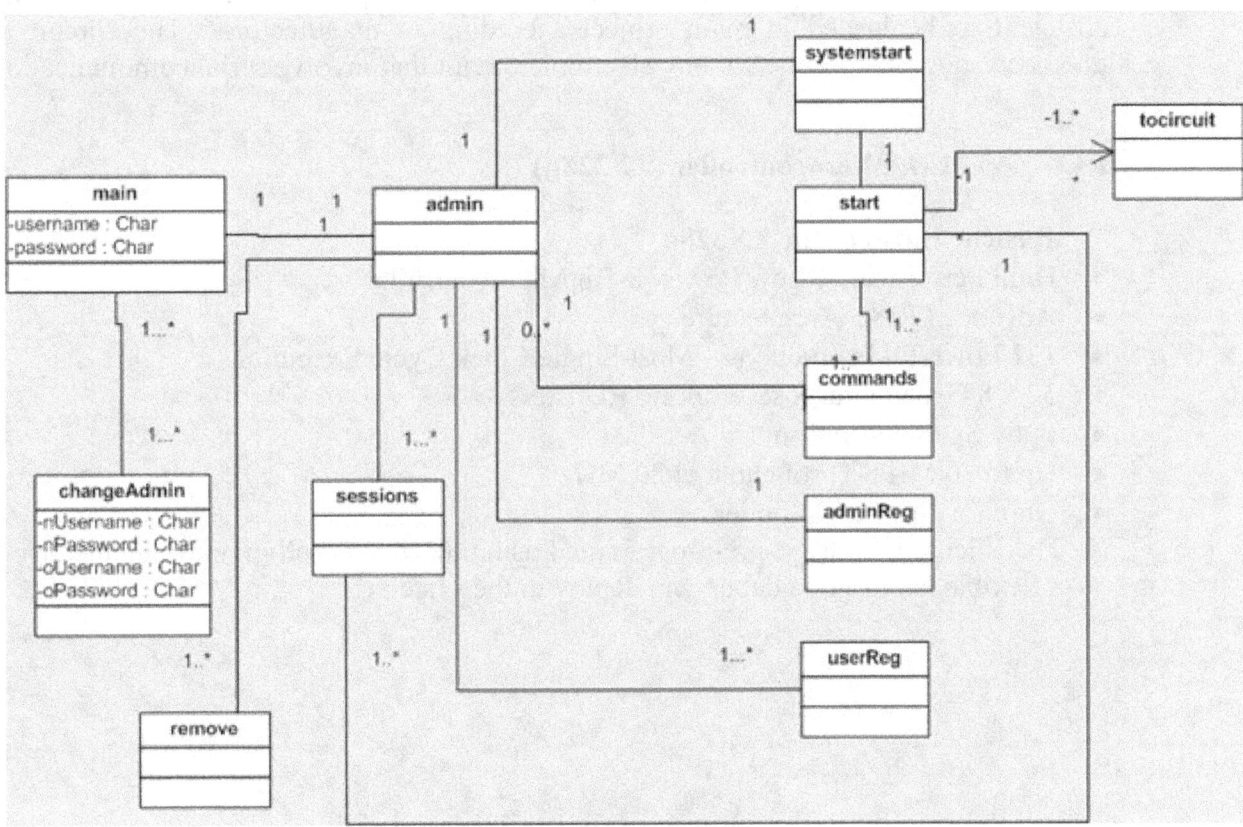

Figure 4: uml class diagram for remc

4.4. SYSTEM FEATURES AND DESIGN

4.4.1. Modem Features

Modem is a device used to receive/send SMS from/to the user mobile phone. Modem identifies the message and passes it to the REMC-HOUSE software for further processing. The modem is capable of using the AT Commands.

4.4.2. Electronic Circuit Features

The electronic circuit consists of the Microcontroller (ZX328n), MAX232 (st232cn), PWM Solenoid/valve driver, a 12V DC fan and 5V LED. Also the passive devices like capacitors, resistors and many others. The Microcontroller uses external oscillator of about 10MHz. The system components are separate as shown below but they can be connected easily but it's not easily to simulate as no any computer and modem to execute the codes. Instead, the connection is so sufficient to be loaded in main project according to manufacturer. The Circuit are pre-designed and suggested for use for any electronic circuit that involve serial communication.

4.4.2.1. ATMEL Microcontroller (ZX328n)

Basic features of the ZX328n
- High Performance, Low Power 8-Bit Microcontroller
- Advanced RISC Architecture
- 131 Powerful Instructions – Most Single Clock Cycle Execution
- 32 x 8 General Purpose Working Registers
- Fully Static Operation
- Up to 20 MIPS Throughput at 20 MHz
- On-chip 2-cycle Multiplier

The Microcontroller is pre-programmed using the ZBasic programming language. This is a flexible language to debug and deploy to the system.

The recommended circuit configuration:

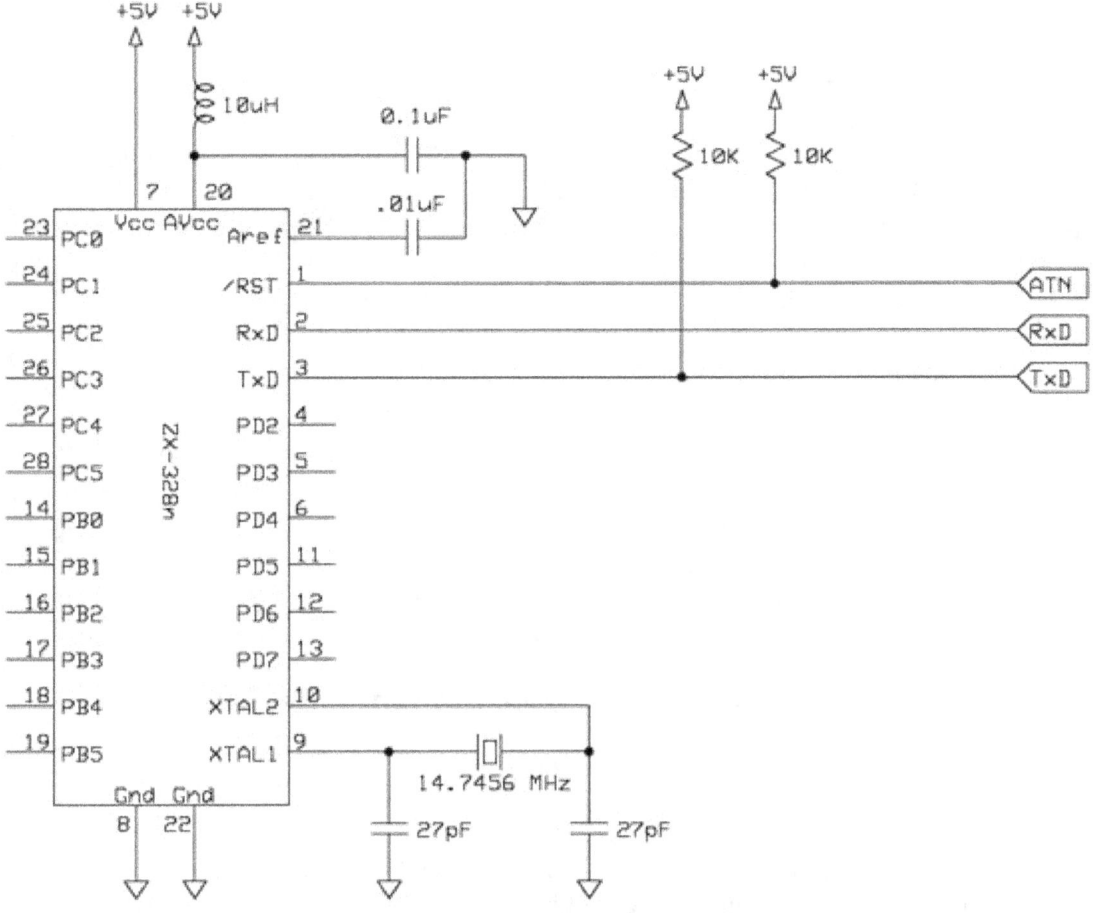

Figure 5 : ZX-328n Circuit configuration

I use the port C of the microcontroller to connect the LEDs and fan. The wires (ATN, RxD and TxD) are connected to the MAX232.

4.4.2.2. Interface between microcontroller and MAX232

Usually, there are about 3 suggested serial interface of the ZX-328n microcontroller according to the manufacturer. But I have chosen the one using the MAX232 as it is a fast and easy to implement the system. Below is the electronic circuit that was suggested in a ZX-328n manufacturer manual.

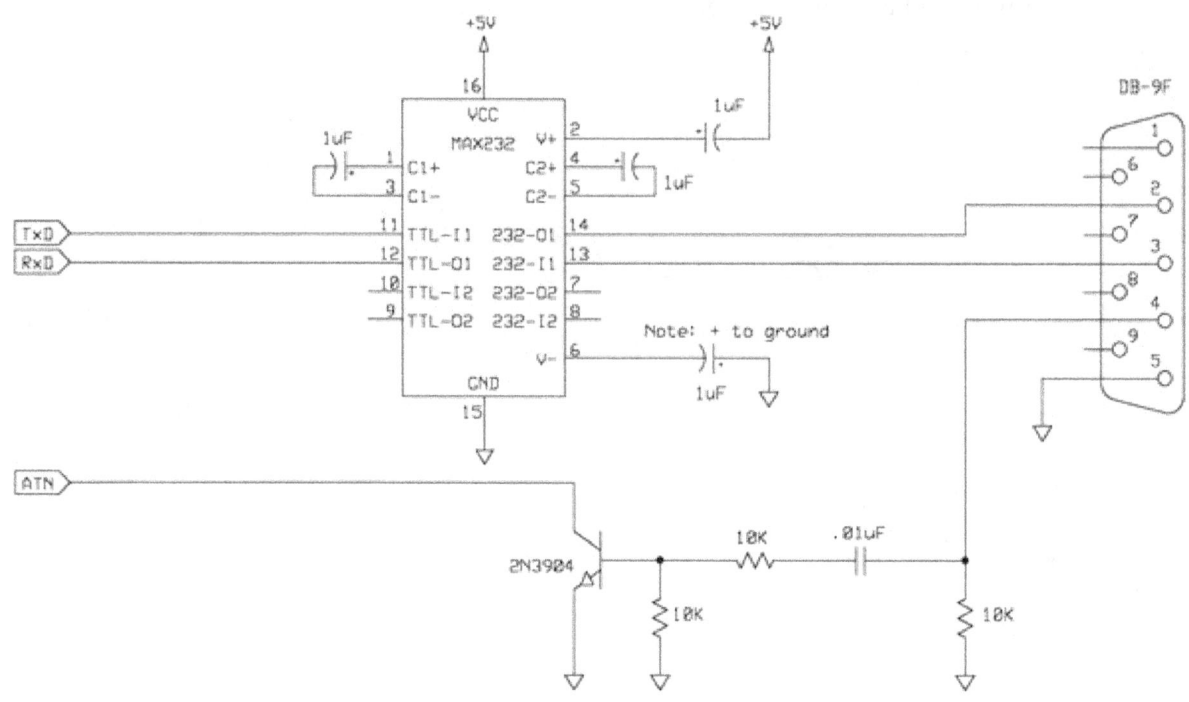

Figure 6: Serial comm. interface for ZX-328n Microcontroller

4.4.2.3. PWM SOLENOID/VALVE DRIVER FOR FANS

This is used for the fans. Through changing the PWM signal, the speed of the fan varies instantly. The driver is very sensitive in DC change as it is connected to the fan and microcontroller.

Basic features of the PWM Solenoid/valve driver
- High output drive: 2.3A
- Wide Supply Range: +9V to +60V
- Complete Function
    - PWM Output
    - Internal 24kHz Oscillator
    - Digital Control Input
    - Adjustable Delay and Duty Cycle
    - Over/Under Current Indicator
- Fully protected
    - Thermal Shutdown with Indicator
    - Internal Current Limit

The suggested circuit configuration according to manufacturer:

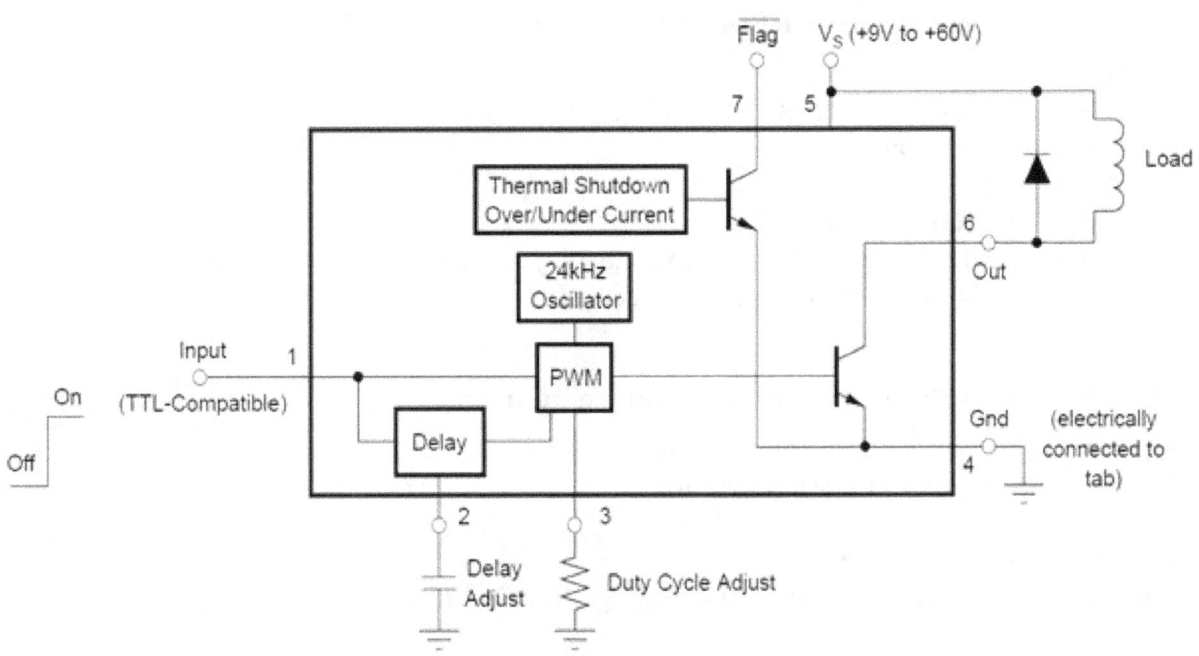

Figure 7 : PWM Solenoid/Valve driver configuration circuit

Actually, the Load (as seen in figure 5) is replaced with 12V DC fan.

4.4.3. REMC-HOUSE SOFTWARE FEATURES

4.4.3.1. Connect to the modem and Microcontroller::SF01

Description
The user sets the port for Modem and Microcontroller and connects

Stimulus/Response Sequences
Preconditions:
- User knows modem's and Microcontroller's port. Modem and Microcontroller mode is on.
- User sets Modem Port
- User sets Microcontroller Port.
- User connects the Modem and Microcontroller.

Post-conditions:
If the system detects the availability of the port will display a message system connected. NOTE: It doesn't mean that the ports connected are as prescribed but the available ports have been connected.

Abnormal Paths:
If the ports are incorrect the system will not work as prescribed. The user should be very careful to avoid this to happen as she/he should read the User Documentation very well.

4.4.3.2. System Feature Show REMC "About" information::SF02
Description
The User chooses to view the REMC "About" information.
Stimulus/Response Sequences
Preconditions: None
    User clicks the about button.
Post conditions: The About information box is displayed showing some information
    About the REMC manufacturer

4.4.3.3. System Feature current session information::SF03
Description
    The User sees the current session executing.

Stimulus/Response Sequences
Preconditions: The system has received a message from the modem

Post conditions: NONE

Functional Requirements
Specializes: SF01

4.4.3.4. System Feature Message sent to Microcontroller::SF04
Description
    The User sees the current message that has been sent to Microcontroller.

Stimulus/Response Sequences
Preconditions: The system has received a message from the modem.

Post conditions: Message shown in a form

Functional Requirements
Specializes: SF03

4.4.3.5. System Feature Notified unauthorized user::SF05
Description
    The User sees the number and a message is sent to authorize user.

Stimulus/Response Sequences
Preconditions: The system has received a message from the modem.

Post conditions: Message shown in a form and the number of the unauthorized user is sent to the authorized user.

Functional Requirements
Specializes: SF06

4.4.3.6. System Feature set a authorized numbers::SF07
Description
   The User sets the number of authorized users.

Stimulus/Response Sequences
Preconditions:
   The User must identify the authorized number and know how to write as prescribed in User documentation.

Post conditions: If any of the number interrupts the system works as instructed.

4.4.3.7. System Feature saves users numbers::SF08
Description
   The User sees the numbers that were using the machine.

Stimulus/Response Sequences
Preconditions: The system has received a message from the modem.
          The system knows the authorized numbers.

Post conditions: The number is saved only on session when the system is ON.

Functional Requirements
Specializes: SF03

4.4.3.8. System Feature Request for last message status::SF09
Description
   The message is sent to users handset describing the last message received

Stimulus/Response Sequences
Preconditions: The system has received a message from the modem.
          The functional message has been received before the request.

Post conditions: Message received in a users hand set.

Functional Requirements
Specializes: SF03

4.4.4. REMC HOUSE SOFTWARE DETAILED DESIGN

4.4.4.1. SYSTEM SOFTWARE(DATABASE) ARCHITECTURE

Most relational database servers are separate applications that run on their own. To interact
With a running relational database, the database vendor provides a database driver. In .NET, a
Database driver is a piece of proprietary code that talks to the relational database server, but
Exposes its functionality using the ADO.NET layer.

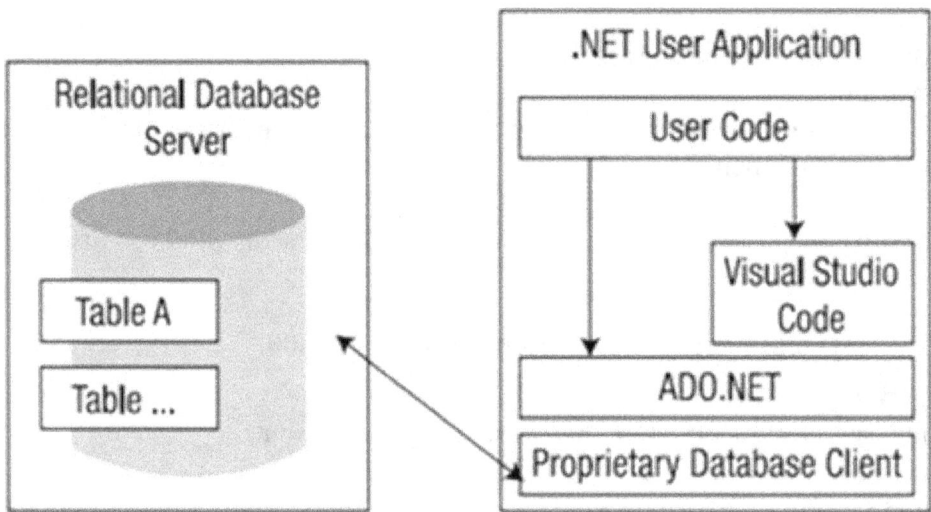

Figure 8 : common database architecture

Since, I have opted to use the Mysql database then I obtained Mysql driver for .NET from Mysql site. I have opted for this architecture since REMC needs to save administrators, users, sessions and system events. Also, I have used XML (Extensible markup language) to save sessions like SMS that are sent and Administrator interactions with the software. I have opted for XML since its architecture is simple in implementation.

4.4.4.2. UML SEQUENCE DIAGRAM

The sequence diagram is used primarily to show the interactions between objects in the sequential order that those interactions occur. One of the primary uses of sequence diagrams is in the transition from requirements expressed as use cases to the next and more formal level of refinement. Use cases are often refined into one or more sequence diagrams.

SCENARIO: Sequence diagram for login into administrative page

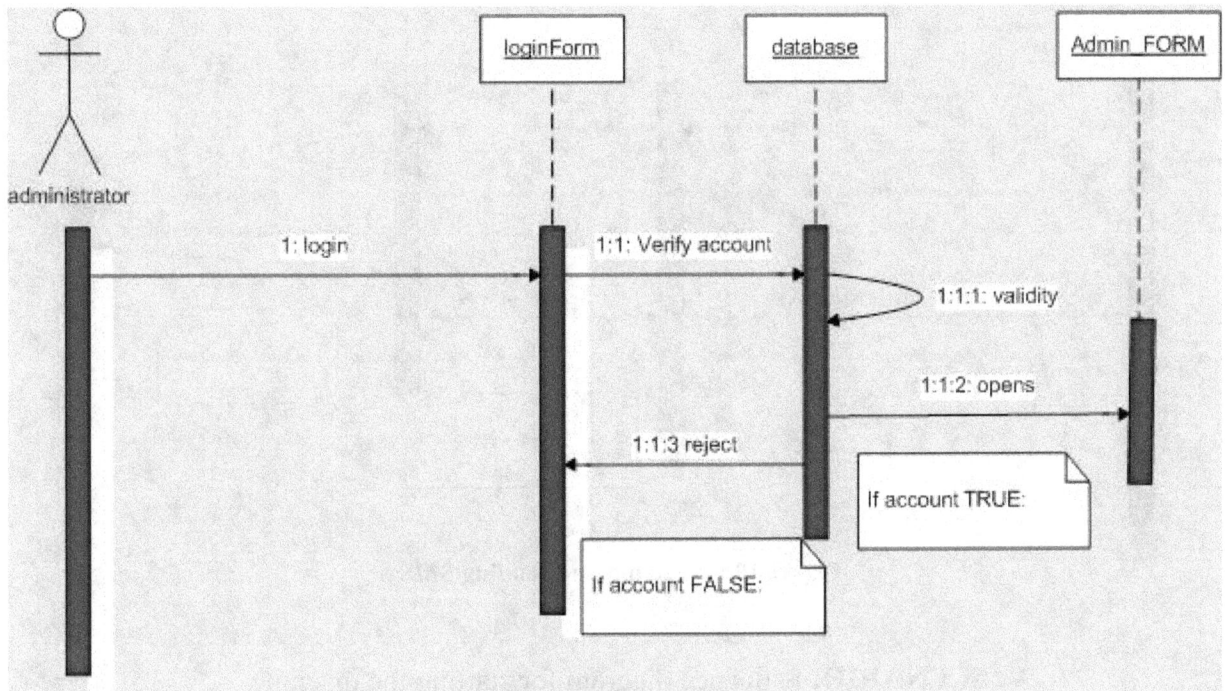

Figure 9 : sequence diagram for administrator login

SCENARIO: Sequence diagram for sending and receiving SMS between modem and circuit

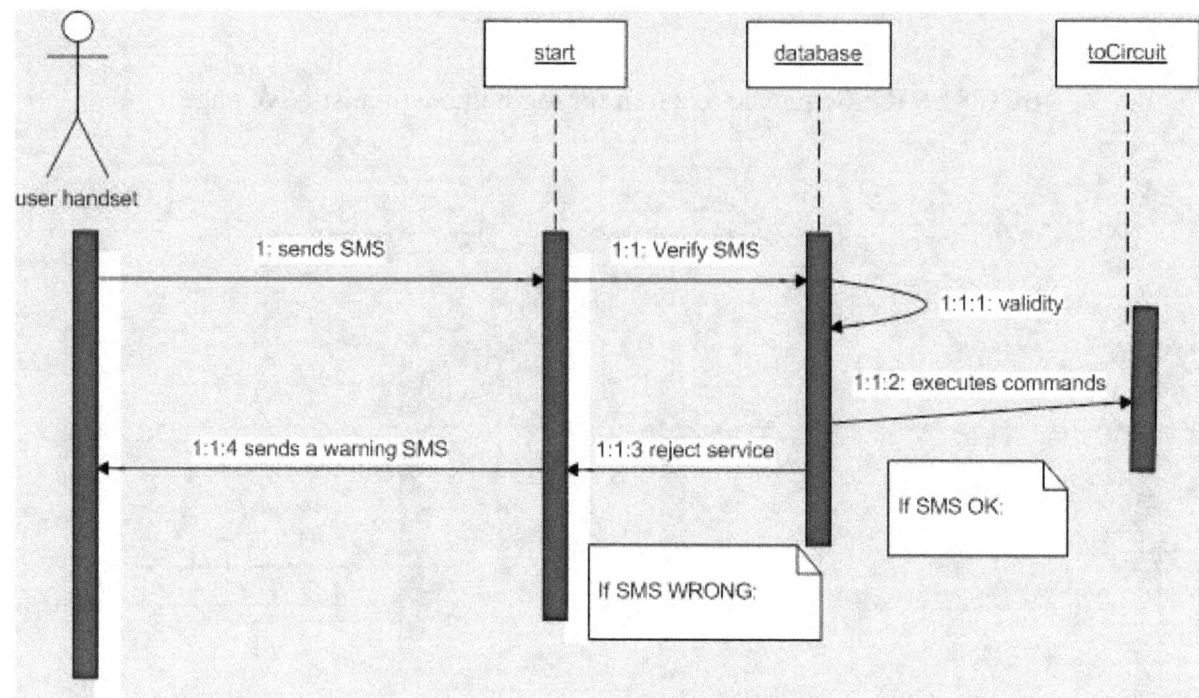

Figure 10 : receiving and sending SMS

SCENARIO: Sequence diagram for starting the machine

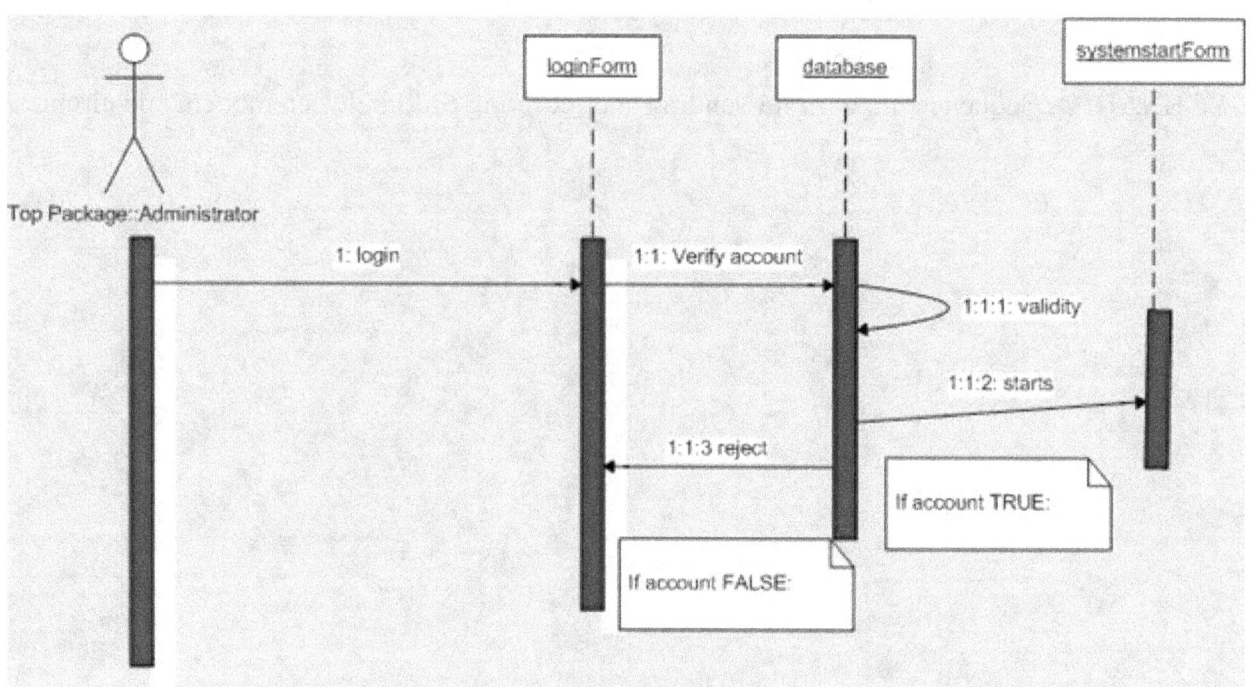

Figure 11: sequence diagram for starting the system

4.4.4.3. UML DESIGN CLASS DIAGRAM

Show the classes of the system, their inter-relationships, and the operations and attributes of the classes. Class diagrams are typically used, although not all at once, to:

- Explore domain concepts in the form of a domain model
- Analyze requirements in the form of a conceptual/analysis model
- Depict the detailed design of object-oriented or object-based software

i) Design class diagram for the program that starts the system

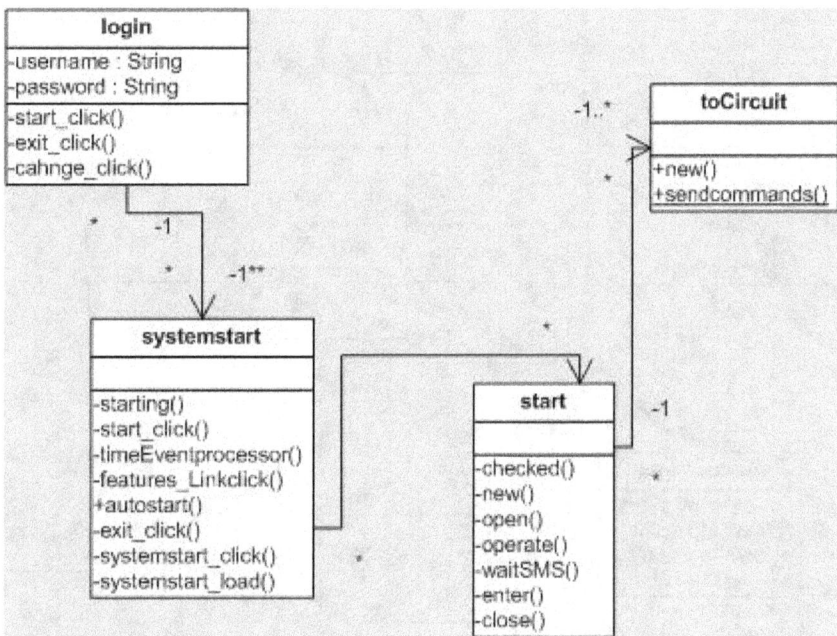

Figure 12 : Design class diagram for starting the system

ii) Design class diagram for the program that allows administrator to change the system parameters.

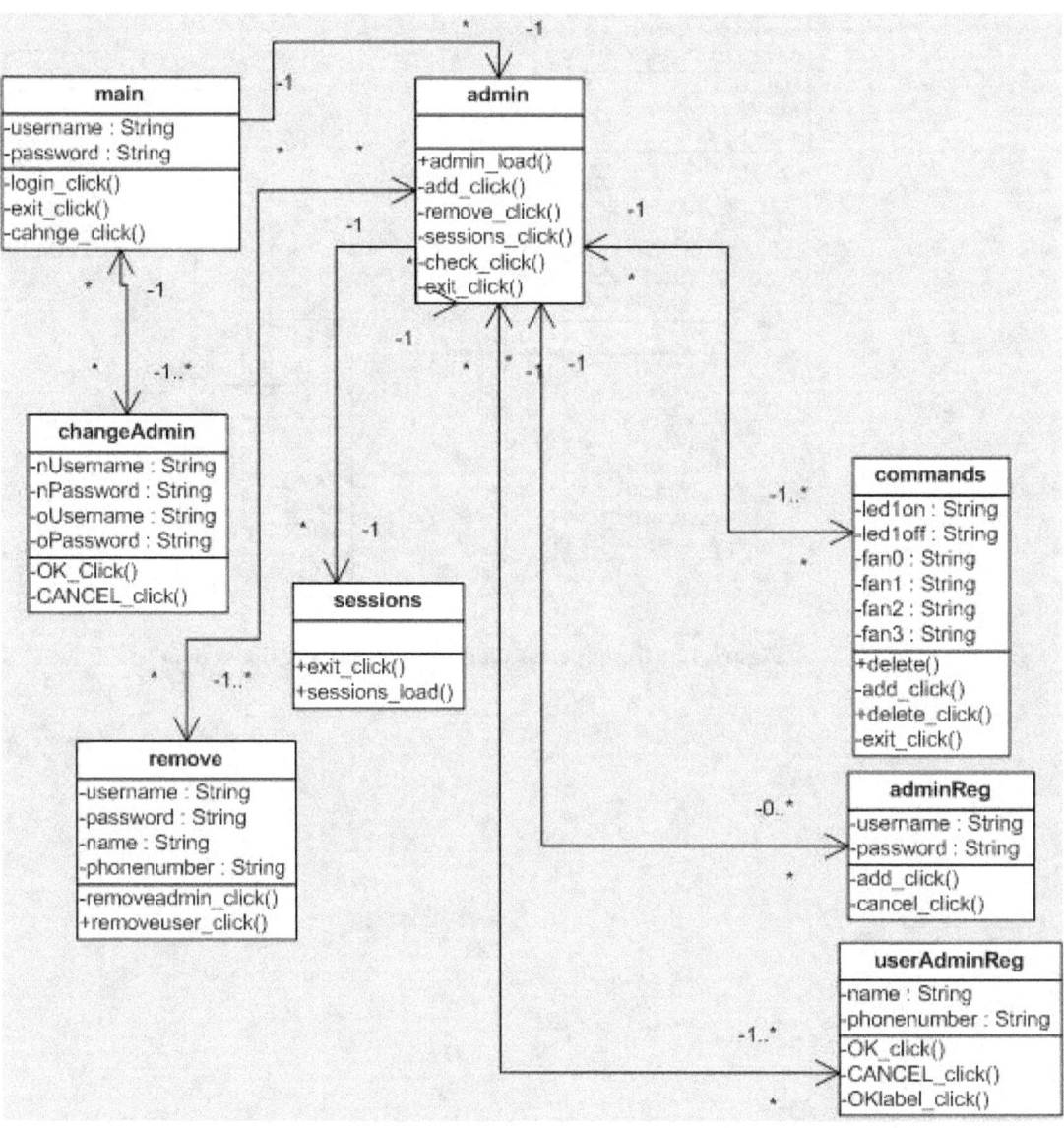

Figure 13 : design class diagram for administrative updates

4.4.4.4. DATABASE DESIGN

ENTITY RELATIONSHIP DIAGRAM

The ERD gives the relationship between all the entities, which are logically related in the system/database. ERD in Figure 12 shows how the entities are related and documented.

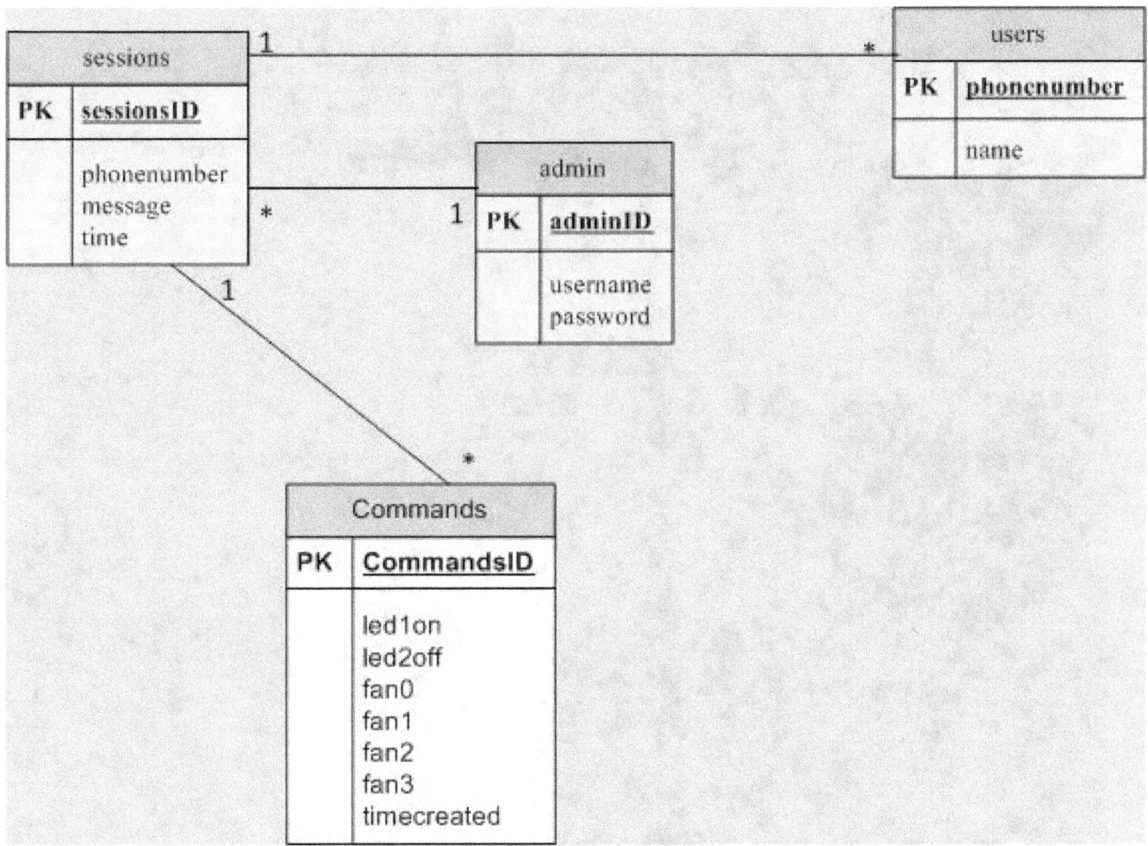

Figure 14 : system's ERD

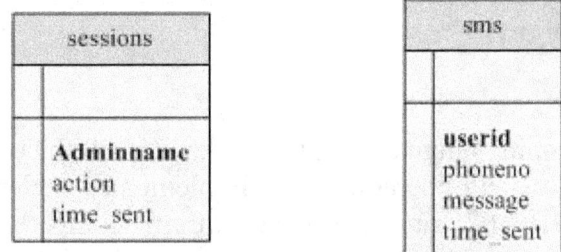

Figure 15: System's XML Template ERD

4.5. IMPLEMENTATION

This initial implementation involved software development and circuit design. Since the circuit is in its preliminary design it's working as planned but the picture included to show the preliminary implementation. I am also going to show some forms of the REMC House software.

The circuit design according to the design

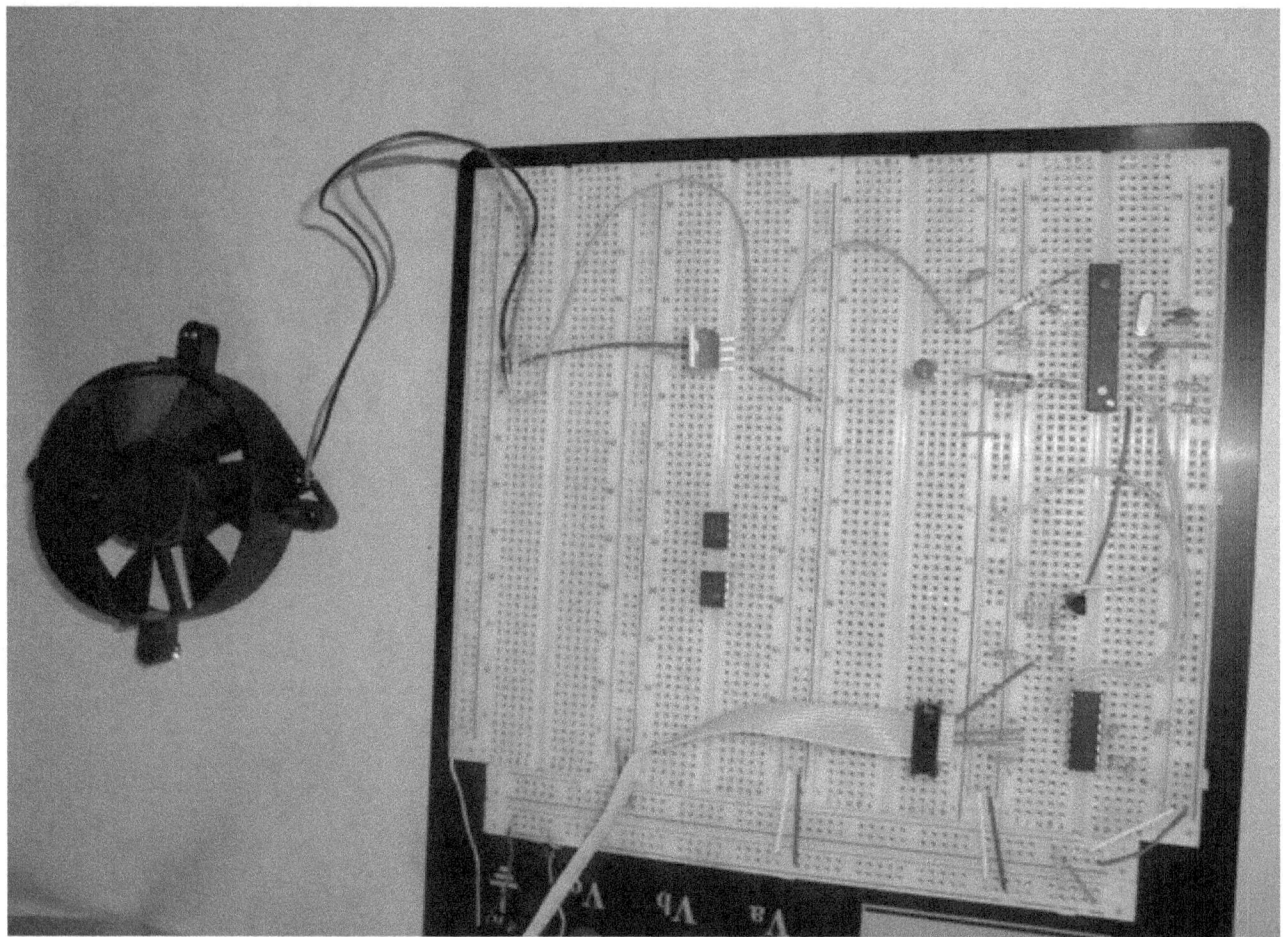

Figure 16 : REMC House electronic circuit

4.5.1. TECHNOLOGIES USED:

1. **VB.NET 2008**

    This programming language is used to develop all the codes and forms concerning the system flow and operations. It's implemented under .NET Framework 3.5v. I have used VB.NET simply because of my competence in this language. But alternatively Java, Visual C# and C++ could suite the work. Also any object oriented language could easily suite the work.

2. XAMPP CONTROL PANEL

This one provides the Mysql that is used to create the essential database for the system. XAMPP stands for apache, php, perl and Mysql. This provides a Mysql database with a bit well performance. Of course any alternative database like oracle or MS SQL server could suite the work.

3. AT COMMANDS

This is an old system commands to communicate with the modem. These are the basis of instructions that could be used to communicate or command the modem. I have used this command to build a low capacity message gateway.

4. XML(Extensible mark-up Language)

Is a set of rules for encoding documents in machine readable form. It is defined in the XML 1.0 Specification produced by the W3C and several other related specifications, all gratis open standard. I have only used this for as an alternative technology for storing some of the messages. Of course simple xml sheets occupy very small space compared when the same data is stored in a database.

5. Microsoft office Excel 2007

Microsoft Excel is a commercial spreadsheet application written and distributed by Microsoft for Microsoft windows and Mac OS X. It features calculation, graphing tools, pivot tables, and a macro programming language called Visual basic for application. I have developed an application that generates these spreadsheets in assumptions that REMC House administrator is familiar with MS Excel 2007. This allows an administrator to have alternative data viewer.

4.5.2. SYSTEM IMPLENTATION TASKS
A. The software to start the system. This is the one that is used to connect modem and circuit to the system.

Both software have the splash screens before reaching the login form

i) Login form

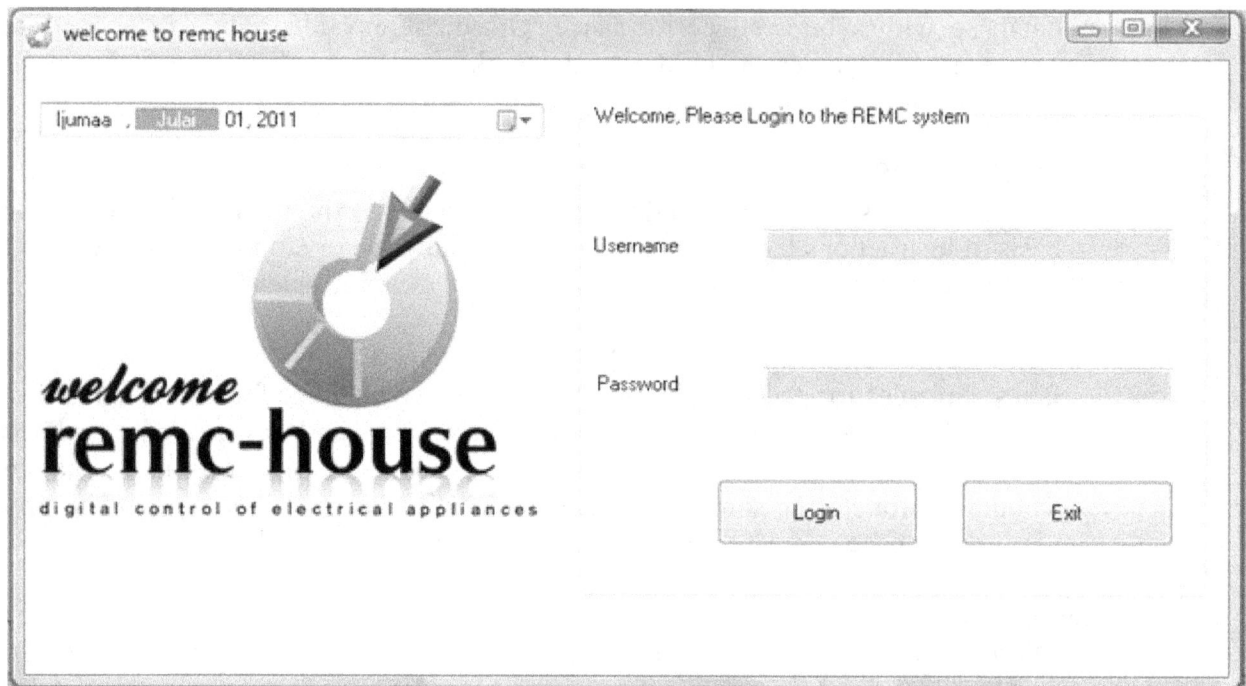

Figure 17: login form for starting the system

Consider there is a mistake in entering the password;

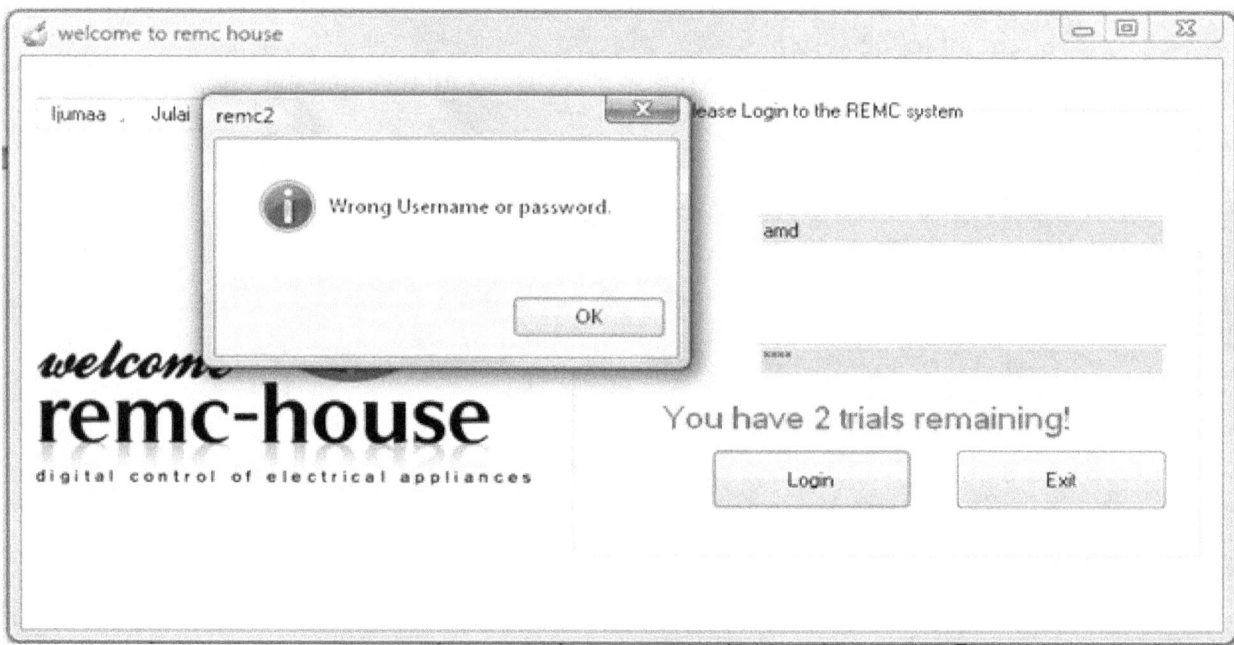

Figure 18 : invalid login warning

ii) When the user clicks OK, then system starts the circuit and modem Activation page.

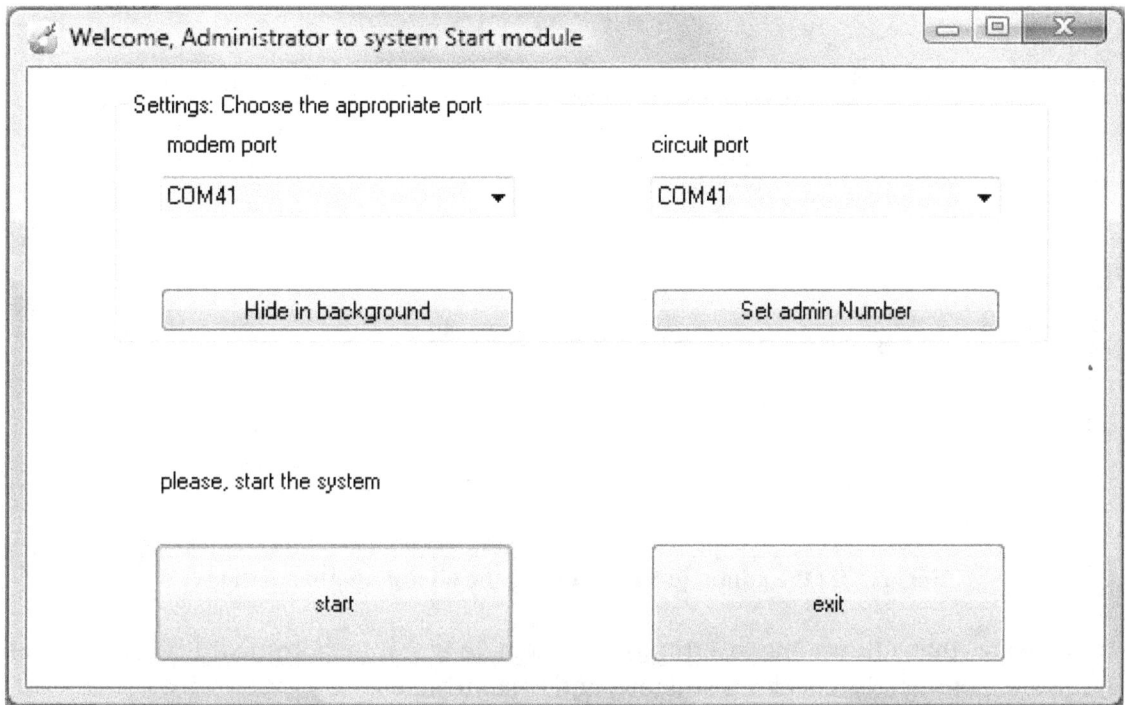

Figure 19 : start system module that connects the modem and the circuit

iii) The software (set admin number) always instructs the user to specify the phone number and ID of the key administrator before starting the system.

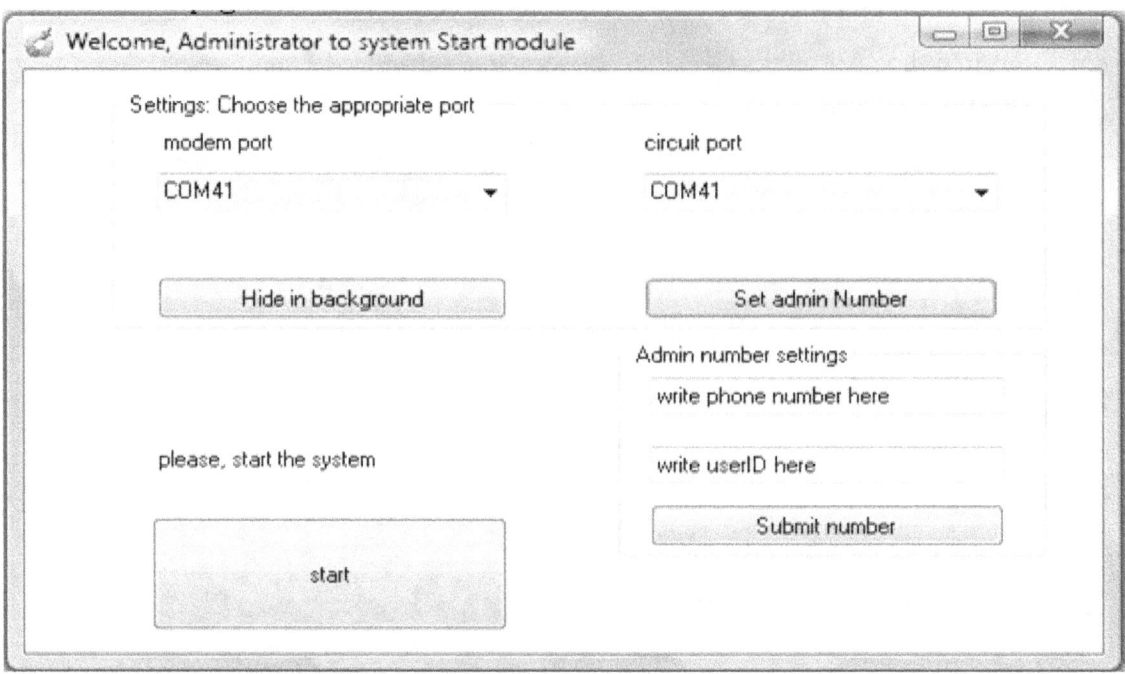

Figure 20 : the admin form displaying the admin number settings

B. The software that allows the user(administrator) to go into administrative privileges like updating users, commands, checking sessions and system states.

a. Login form for administrator

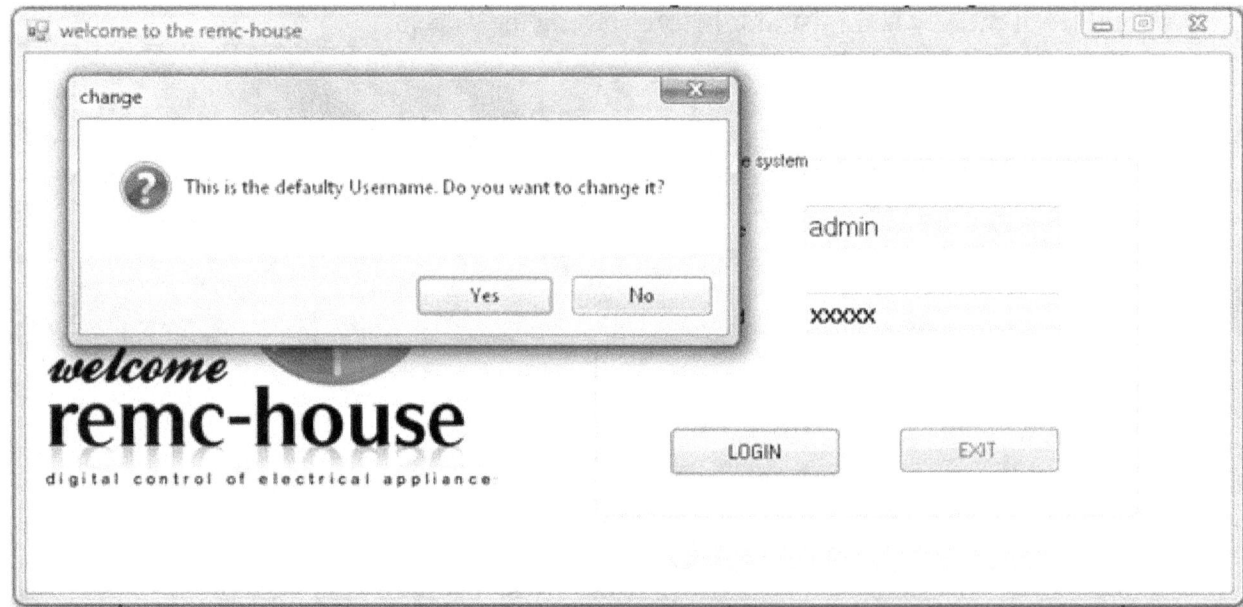

Figure 21 : login form for administrator

b. If login was successfully, the administrative form comes on after you have rejected the request to change the default admin authentication. The admin page has several options that allow the admin to manipulate the system parameters like updating new users and administrators, checking sms sessions (received sms), sent sms logs, updating the commands and check the about and online/local help.

Figure 22 : administrative form for system service options

c. I have developed sessions and check commands form.

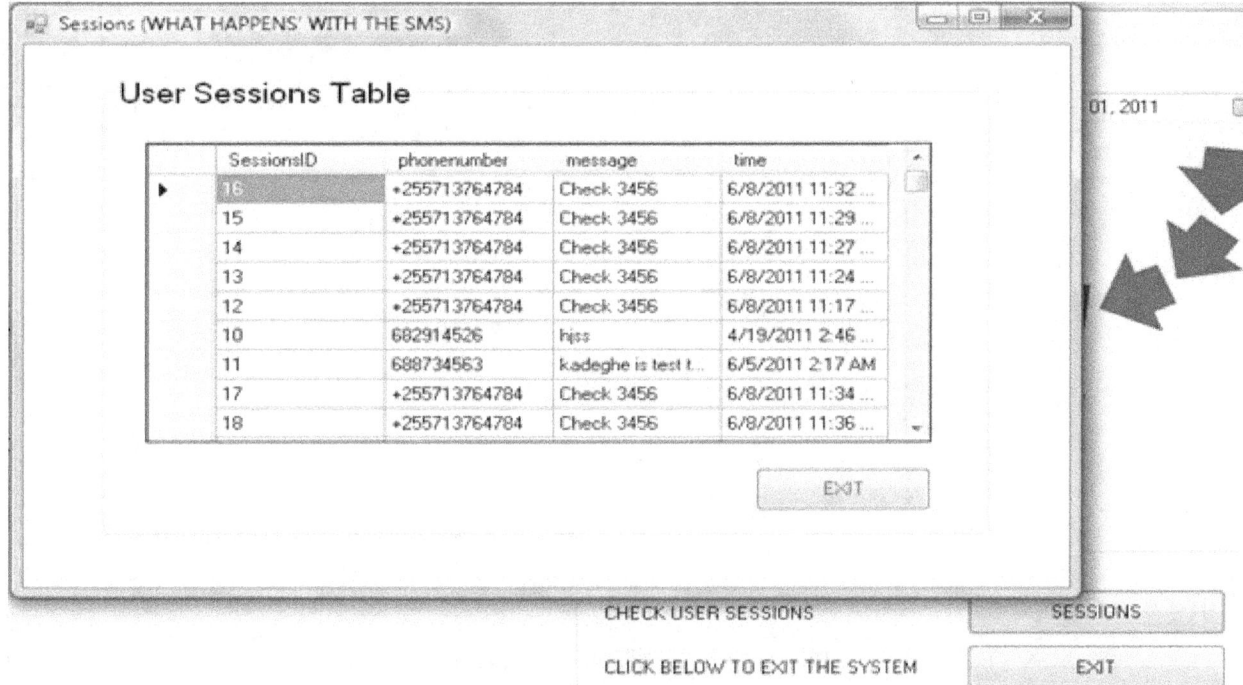

Figure 23 : user interruption table or sessions

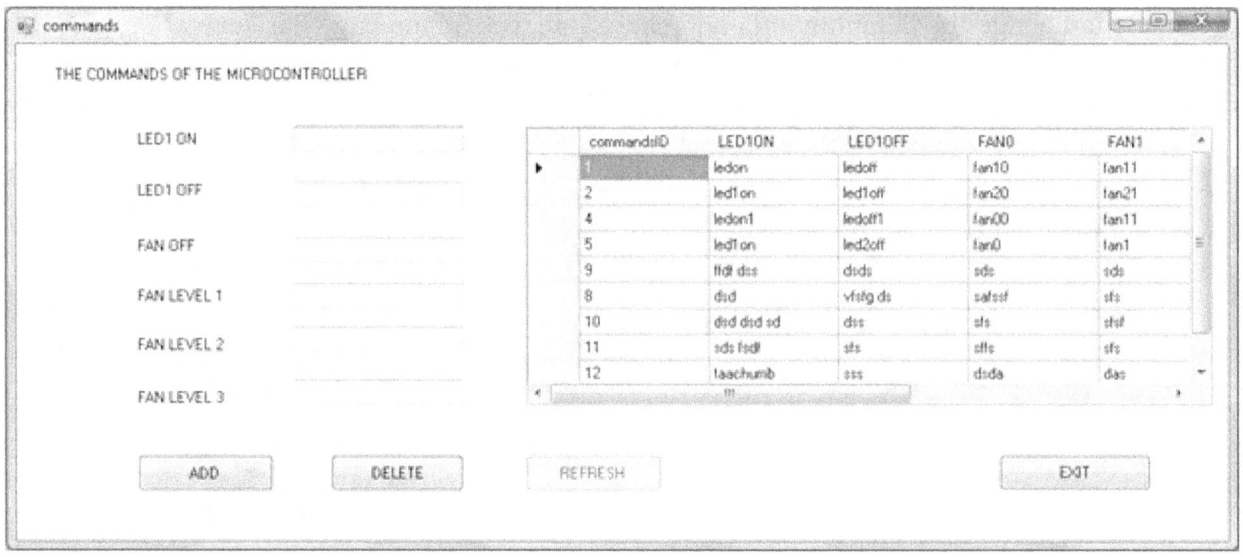

Figure 24 : command table and updates form

d. In login form there is a command that allows to change administrator password and username, if clicked the form change will show up;

In case, the username or password was incorrect then the system allows to 2 last chances before it quits completely in attempt to prevent anonymous attempts.

Figure 25 : invalid change when performed

36

e. Adding normal users is a normal act, but attempt to add a full control administrator is a risky task. The system takes care as shown below

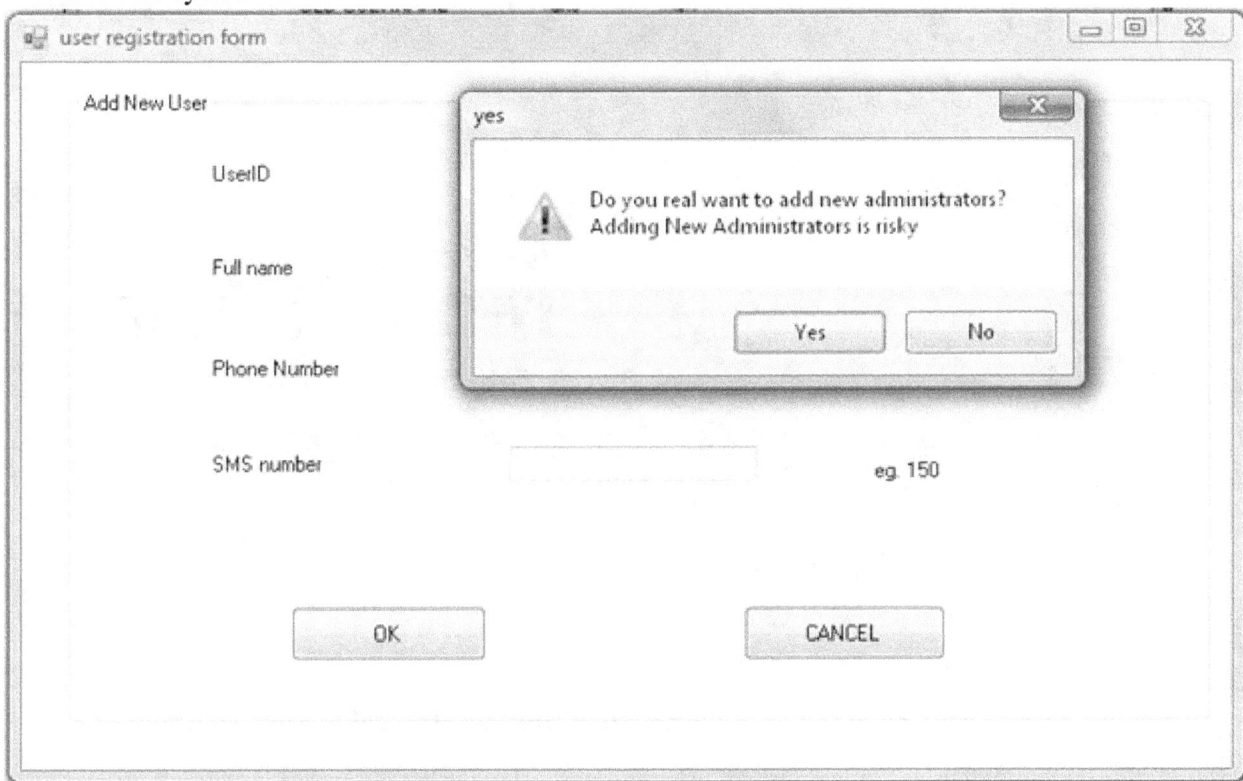

Figure 26: Attempt to add new administrators

f. Removing both users and administrator could be easy task if you know all the details. But if you don't know them then system instructs you to see using master login functionality.

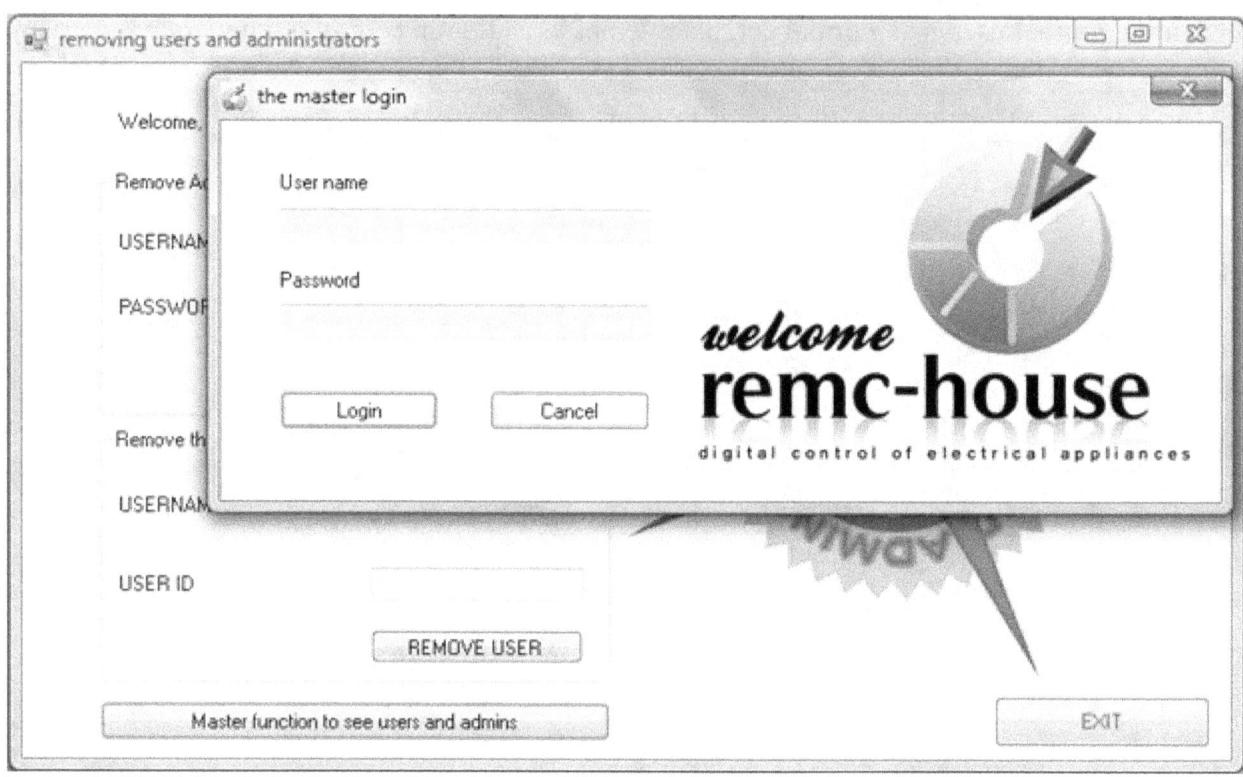

Figure 27: accessing the master login functionality of the system

g. Export data from either xml or database to Excel file

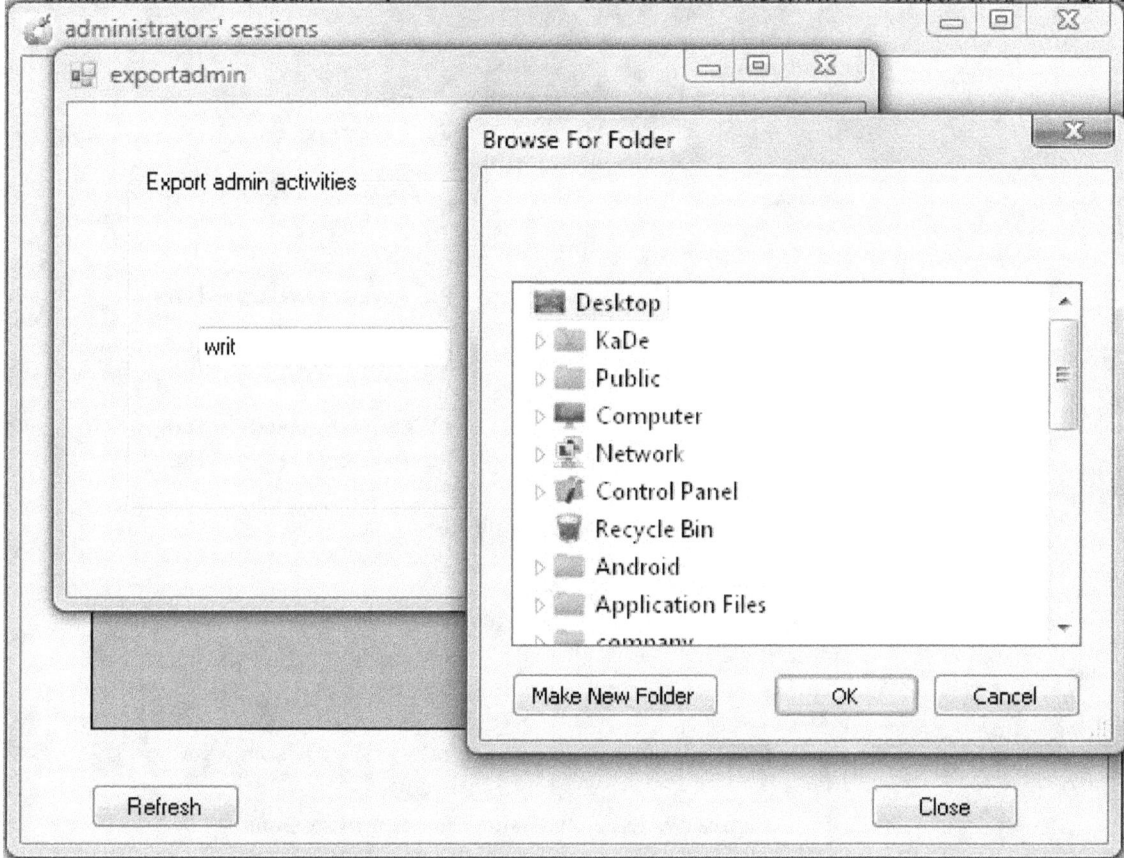

Figure 28: Exporting admin sessions to excel file

If it's successful created then the created file of excel has the following view if opened. The user is left with the task of editing it before printing.

	A	B	C	D
1		Admin name	Operations	Time Recorded
2		admin	Successfully Login	7/1/2011 17:56
3		adm	1st unSuccessfully masterLogin	7/1/2011 17:57
4		admin	Successfully Login	7/1/2011 18:15
5		previous	Clicked to see the critical remove form	7/1/2011 18:15
6			1st unSuccessfully masterLogin	7/1/2011 18:15
7		admin	Successfully masterLogin	7/1/2011 18:15
8		previous	Clicked to see the systems sessions form	7/1/2011 18:15
9		kade	Successfully Login	7/1/2011 18:19
10		previous	Clicked to see the critical remove form	7/1/2011 18:19
11		admin	Successfully masterLogin	7/1/2011 18:19
12		previous	Clicked to see the systems sessions form	7/1/2011 18:19
13		previous	Clicked to see the systems sessions form	7/1/2011 18:19
14			1st unSuccessfully masterLogin	7/1/2011 18:20
15		admin	Successfully masterLogin	7/1/2011 18:20
16		previous	Clicked to see the systems sessions form	7/1/2011 18:20
17		previous	Clicked to see the leave the admin softv	7/1/2011 18:21
18		admin	Successfully Login	7/1/2011 18:26
19		previous	Clicked to see the critical remove form	7/1/2011 18:26
20		admin	Successfully masterLogin	7/1/2011 18:26
21		previous	Clicked to see the systems sessions form	7/1/2011 18:26
22		previous	Clicked to see the leave the admin softv	7/1/2011 18:27
23		admin	Successfully Login	7/1/2011 18:29

Figure 29: Excel 2007 sheet for admin sessions

Those are few window forms of the REMC House. Practically, REMC House has a lot of forms and files that are interconnected to accomplish REMC House objectives. These forms can easily be explored using your computer when remc is installed.

h. Database that is used by remc house

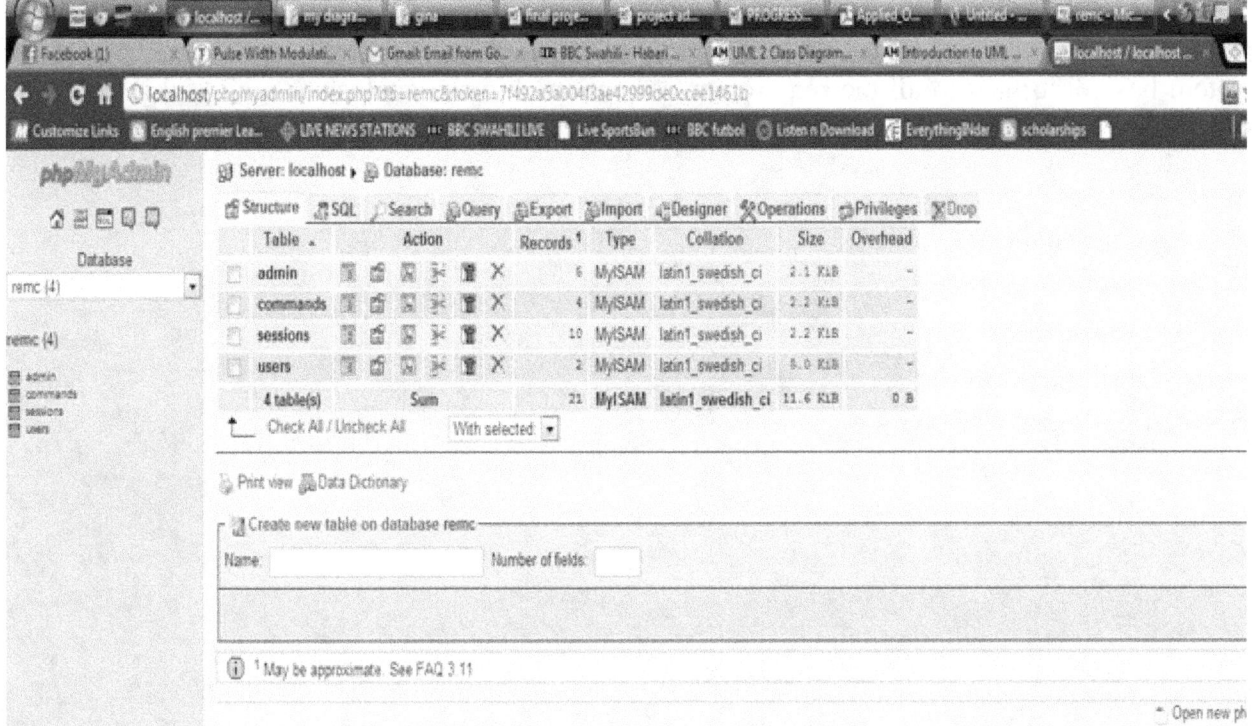

Figure 30 : remc database in phpmyadmin

4.6. SYSTEM TESTING

This is the last stage of the system development. In this step, the system was tested to identify errors as well as make corrections in case of any error before it has reached to the users.

The system has two distinct parts that were tested separately. These parts are hardware or circuit and software. All of them have conformed to user requirements.

REMC-SOFTWARE

This is the software that governs system operations. It has a part that receives messages saves them and send them to the microcontroller. This software was tested and some very small errors were found. Though it has never received a brutal test as needed due to shortage of time.

REMC-HARDWARE

This is the hardware or circuit that controls external devices that are connected to the system. Practically, it would have involved so many devices but this model has very few connections to simplify design perspective. All of them have been tested but there some problems still with it. These problems have not appeared to disturb the circuit severely but rather they occur very occasionally.

All other supporting features of the system were tested as they were created, and the whole system was tested by entering different values in different situations and the system worked fine. After all the tests carried above, there is no any serious error which has been detected, since the system has conformed to all the requirements mentioned in the analysis stage. At this point the system is ready to be used as intended i.e. Deploying.

CHAPTER 5

5. CONCLUSIONS

5.1. USER REQUIREMENTS

The system has covered all the requirements as evaluated in Software specifications document. These requirements have originated from the project objectives. This has satisfied/met the requirement for remote switching of electrical devices in a house using SMS.

5.2. EFFECTIVENESS

This system is relative good especially in producing reports of its sessions, admin sessions and SMS sessions. Also, the system is good in accepting remote commands that are subjected to command the electrical devices. This system can conclusively be accepted as a remote control of electrical devices that uses SMS.

The system is also good in receiving admin commands like adding users and administrators. Generally, the system software is more effective compared to its interfaces between Modem to computer and computer to circuit. These interfaces don't perform as expected though there is no any adverse effect could easily be recognised by the user.

5.3. LEARNABILITY

Can the admin or user accomplish the set of tasks made to the system?
YES, since the system is very simple and easy to use.
The system is based in well organized forms and modules. Every task could be twisted to its desirability. The admin can control the system while users can do chat with the system easily using very simple words that controls the system. Simply, its takes very short time to learn the system functionalities and starting exploring them.

5.4. RECOMMENDATIONS

I recommend REMC House as the alternative remote control technology for most homes. This system is sited for further improvements mostly in its software part. Hardware is not that much important as compared to Software part which seems to provide a lot of functionalities.

5.5. CONCLUSION EVALUATION

The system has met all its specified objectives. Also its implementation has provided alternatives for accomplishing these objectives.

The system can't be installed directly to the house before evaluating client's needs. Actually, this system act like a model to the actual system. Its techniques are relevant to implement a real system to a site.

Through this development I have realised several ways to integrate technology using quite a lot of technologies leading to a challenging work while being very resourceful.

6. REFERENCE

"How Your Home's Electrical System Works". 2000 - 2010, Acme Parts.com.
   http://www.acmehowto.com/howto/homemaintenance/electrical/overview.php

"Remote control".2010 Wikimedia Foundation, Inc.
http://en.wikipedia.org/wiki/Remote_control

"ZX-328n Microcontroller".2010 Elba Corp.
http://www.zbasic.net/

Electrical Safety foundation international (ESFI), 2008. Electrical safety workbook.
http://www.fnal.gov/pub/takefive/documents/Elec%20Safety%20Workbook.pdf

"Event driven programming". 2011 Wikimedia foundation, Inc.
http://en.wikipedia.org/wiki/Event-driven_programming

David Luckham: *The Power of Events - An Introduction to Complex Event Processing in Distributed Enterprise Systems*, Addison-Wesley, ISBN 0-201-72789-7.

7. APPENDIX

A. FORM: QUESTIONNAIRE FOR REMC HOUSE SYSTEM

1. What services do you prefer to be offered by REMC HOUSE (Please tick your Choices)
   - ☐ Opening automatic fence gate
   - ☐ Switching ON/OFF the lights
   - ☐ Using SMS to interrupt with REMC house system
   - ☐ Using TCP/IP to interrupt with REMC-House
   - ☐ Switching ON/OFF the fans
   - ☐ Reporting house movements and fire outbreak
   - ☐ Control all electronic and electrical devices in a house.

2. What other services do you prefer to be offered by REMC-HOUSE?
   a. _____
   b. _____
   c. _____
   d. _____
   e. _____

3. Would you prefer to use the REMC-HOUSE to give total control of electrical device in your house?
   - ☐ Yes
   - ☐ No

4. Would you prefer to use the REMC-HOUSE to recharge your LUKU in your home?
   - ☐ Yes
   - ☐ No

5. Would you prefer to use the REMC-HOUSE to be PC based or stand alone system?
   - ☐ Yes, both
   - ☐ No, only PC based
   - ☐ No, only stand alone system

6. Are you able to afford cost of electricity of about 2.5 units per day that is 500Tshs that will consumed by REMC-HOUSE? (Note: it costs about 15,000Tshs per month). *This is an approximation figure.(Might vary)*
   - ☐ Yes
   - ☐ No

7. Do you see any relevant practical use of REMC-House to a Tanzanian normal life and their homes?
   - ☐ Yes
   - ☐ No

B. TIME SCHEDULE OF Phase II

S/N	ACTIVITIES	Phase II														
	WEEKS	1	2	3	4	5	6	7	8	9	10	11	12	13	14	15
1	Activity one	■	■	■	■	■	■	■								
2	Activity two			■	■	■	■	■	■	■	■	■	■	■		
3	Activity three							■	■	■	■	■	■	■		
4	Activity four													■	■	■
5	Activity five														■	■
6	Activity six	■	■	■	■	■	■	■	■	■	■	■	■	■	■	■

KEY:

Activity one: Redesigning the project classes and design classes

Activity two: development of the codes and interfaces

Activity three: design and implementation the circuit and its interface

Activity Four: System testing (verification and validation)

Activity five: development of the system documentation and user manual

Activity six: Literature review

NB: The week 1, 2 and 3 were used for first semester. So apparently the first Phase work was done in those weeks.

C. TIME SCHEDULE OF Phase I

Table 1 : Table of activities.

S/N	ACTIVITIES	Phase I														
	WEEKS	1	2	3	4	5	6	7	8	9	10	11	12	13	14	15
1	Activity one	■	■	■												
2	Activity two			▨	▨	▨	▨	▨	▨							
3	Activity three							■	■	■	■	■	■	■	■	■
4	Activity four									▨	▨	▨	▨	▨	▨	▨
5	Activity five	■	■	■	■	■	■	■	■	■	■	■	■	■	■	■

KEY:

Activity one: Decision on the project title and submission.

Activity two: Review and hypothesis on the general Remote control systems available.

Activity three: Prioritizing the functional requirements and the key components Needed in system.

Activity Four: Analyzing and Designing the REMC-HOUSE systems.

Activity five: Literature review

NB: The week 13, 14 and 15 were postponed to week 1, 2 and 3 of the second phase.

www.ingramcontent.com/pod-product-compliance
Lightning Source LLC
Chambersburg PA
CBHW080840170526
45158CB00009B/2592